speakership

Matt Church
Col Fink
Sacha Coburn

th◉ught leaders

Published by Thought Leaders Publishing

Thought Leaders Publishing
2B, 3-9 Kenneth Street
Manly Vale NSW 2093

First published in 2015
Reprinted in 2017
This edition 2022

ISBN: 978-0-9874708-8-1

Design & typesetting by Michael Fink
Produced for the publisher by exlibris.com.au

Contents

About the authors

Matt Church
mattchurch.com

Matt Church is one of Australia's most enduring and successful motivational speakers. He has been named Speaker of the Year and Educator of the Year by the National Speakers Association, and named in the top ten motivational speakers world-wide. He is generous with his knowledge and is the mentor behind many of the world's leading non-fiction business authors and professional speakers. Matt lives in Sydney, Australia and continues to write, speak and teach the art of oration through various programs for aspiring leaders. In 2001 he founded an international education business, Thought Leaders Global, dedicated to helping clever people be commercially smart. He is the chairman of the business and spends his time developing curriculum and inspiring great thinking and great conversations.

Col Fink
colfink.com

Col Fink spent his childhood as a professional actor and his early career as a stage musician, so he has always felt at home in the spotlight. A mechanical engineer with a masters degree in marketing and data analytics, Col lives at the interface of art and science. After turning his hobby into a career by building a tribe of followers worldwide in a niche sport (kart racing), he became obsessed with the creation and curation of powerful and successful tribes and cultures. His role as the Chief Engagement Officer of Thought Leaders Global allows him to pursue that goal enthusiastically, assisting others build cultures that inspire; in professional, sporting and not-for-profit environments. He speaks regularly about the strategic design and curation of culture, and teaches leadership skills to enable the realisation of cultural aspirations.

Sacha Coburn
sachacoburn.com

Sacha Coburn is a New Zealand based speaker who combines her love of coaching other leaders to speakership mastery with active involvement in leading her own company, Coffee Culture. Sacha heads up the franchise division and walks her talk every day delivering messages that matter. As a conference speaker, Sacha specialises in keynotes and workshops that focus on fearlessness, and leadership from the inside out. She is loved as much for her vulnerability and humour as her hard hitting 'reality check' messages about what it takes to succeed. As a training consultant Sacha has spent over 20 years coaching and developing people and teams. Her obsession with unlocking the latent potential within everyone to be a captivating public speaker has transformed the way thousands of people stand and deliver.

Manifesto

'Speakership is leadership. Every time you speak in public,
you are auditioning for a leadership position'

— James C Humes,
US Presidential speechwriter

Speakership—the art of oration and the science of influence—is the new leadership imperative. Whether you want to increase your leadership credentials to grow your career; or build your communication skills as the head of your business to motivate staff and compel your clients; or deliver keynotes from stage to make public speaking your profession, this book was written for you.

We believe that speakership is the missing link between strategy and execution, between wanting to have people do something and inspiring them to take action. This book is a map for leaders who want to harness the power of presentations to influence their projects, their ideas, and their tribe.

In this book you will find;

- the reasons to get great at speaking;

- the roadmap to achieving it;

- the frameworks and exercises required, and;

- a path to incredible personal growth.

It's a book we hope will provoke you into action. Too many people with so much to offer flirt with the idea of spreading great ideas through powerful speaking, and then are overcome with the enormity of the task. Daunted by the lift that is required to get good at leadership speaking. We hope to inspire and encourage you to do more. Our great hope is that after reading this book, you feel prepared to stretch and challenge yourself, and to think more deeply about the leverage you can gain by being a leader who speaks. At the same time you will leave a lasting positive impact on the people around you and the world at large.

Communication has become one of the most puzzling paradoxes of our time. We live in a world that is hyper-connected; more plugged in, tuned in, turned on than ever before. Everything we need to know is just a swipe away on a mobile device the size of your hand that has more computing power than NASA used to put two men on the moon in 1969! Want to know the temperature in Brazil right now? The price of corn in Maine? How about finding an old friend from high school? Most likely they are just a google search away. The world has irrevocably shrunk.

And yet, social scientists tell us that more and more people feel isolated and disconnected from their communities. They feel overworked, underpaid, misunderstood, and alone. Despite the capability to be 'in touch' twenty four hours a day, seven days a week, many people are disengaged and disillusioned. Business leaders know the struggle to engage and empower a workforce that clocks in, then checks out.

The irony is that our ability to communicate is most likely the single biggest contributor to the success of mankind. The capacity for speech marked our key strategic advantage over the rest of the animal kingdom. Each generation was able to learn from the lessons of their forebears, giving them a head start on survival that led to humans becoming the dominant predator in almost every ecosystem on the planet. And yet, word of mouth wasn't scalable. It was a cumbersome one-to-one, or one-to-few process that was limited by the amount of information that could be reliably transferred from one single mind to another. The pace of innovation and development was inexorably slow.

The evolution of the written word was the catalyst for an enormous shift in human potential. Suddenly a single author could disseminate their ideas widely, and each reader was free to create, innovate, and develop ideas built on the work of generations of scholars and inventors who had gone before. A literate person could learn by early adulthood what had previously taken a whole lifetime to learn, and then devote the rest of their lives to exploring and expanding a body of knowledge.

About 110,000 generations passed between our ancestors who used stone tools, and those who learnt to control fire. Another 20,000 generations lived and died before the Sumerians developed reading and writing. Just 250 generations later, an evolutionary blink after the invention of literacy, Neil Armstrong stepped onto the moon. The pace of human development is accelerating at an exponential rate. It's sobering to imagine what might be achieved within just 5 or 10 generations of the birth of the internet. Colonies on other planets, renewable energy sources providing almost unlimited power at low cost; possibly even the development of medical science to the point where humans can choose not to die.

The nature of the society we live in is radically changing. Easy access to information has transformed the world and continues to enable progress at lightning speed. With history recording the successes and failures of every field of human endeavour, we are no longer limited by the amount of information that can be remembered and passed on by word of mouth. The internet makes it easier than ever before to test and discard bad ideas.

We are living in exciting times! And yet, many of our organisations are crippled by indecision, lack of leadership, and lack of clear direction and vision. This trickles down to an employee base that seems unmotivated, disinterested and transient. To say we have a crisis of engagement is to understate the problem.

The challenge faced by many organisations is the uncertainty and complexity of their commercial reality. They're developing 5 year strategic plans when even the best data analysis doesn't have sufficient predictive power to show us what the changing landscape will look like. We can make educated decisions for the next 12- 36 months, but beyond that? Anything could happen, and most probably will. Executives are juggling the tightrope of expensive risk-taking with the potential pain of missing the boat on the next big thing. In this Age of Disruption, no industry is safe: computer companies are eating the record labels for breakfast, highly educated and ambitious low-cost workers are transforming traditional safe houses like law and accounting. Magazine publishing? Taxi cabs? It's tough.

If that's the bad news, the good news is that opportunity is all around us. Everywhere we look. It's never been more possible to create work worth doing. The stories of successful start-ups, the philanthropic endowments of some of the world's wealthiest, the innovative ways that more and more people are providing products in new and inspiring ways, these things fill us with hope and confidence. But make no mistake, it's a jungle out there!

Speakership is the key to inspiring teams to seize new opportunities, and motivate people through change and disruption. Use it well and you will show confidence as a leader, increase collaboration amongst your teams and ultimately become the personal catalyst that kickstarts progress on those big change initiatives.

Embed speakership in your organisation and you will reduce silos and increase knowledge sharing. It gives you the ability to shape both internal culture and external perceptions, positively promoting the business with powerful memes. Speakership sets the pace of the business; it's how you energise people to act.

When your best people lead out loud, you can stake a claim to territory in the market and build a reputation as thought leaders. Ultimately, you can shift from a business to a brand by becoming an integral part of the cultural landscape. It enables your people to achieve success on the triple bottom line; commercially, professionally, and socially.

So in this cauldron of competition, volatility, and constant change, what are the essentials for survival? Who are the employees, the managers, the executives, the entrepreneurs that can bridge the gap between the struggles of today and the possibility of a brighter future ahead? The leaders of yesterday who hide behind their memos, and flow charts, their tick boxes and the big door of the corner office, simply won't make it. They are managers, not leaders. But we don't need more managers.

We believe that the future won't only belong to the idealists, and the visionaries. Not only to the venture-funded capitalists and their teenage techies. The leaders of today who will take us into an unknown tomorrow will not rely solely on the modern technological tools that have created this feeling of disconnection and ennui. Instead, they'll draw on the early strategies of our ancestors that led to our ultimate success. They will share stories, navigate change, create energy and map out paths for others.

Speakership is the new leadership imperative, and it's based on old fashioned high-touch leadership. Don't inform; inspire.

Speakership is leading out loud. Personable and accessible leaders, influencing and inspiring their people to action by sharing messages that matter. Speakership is the partnership of powerful memes and masterful oration.

For all the incredible discoveries that the written word has enabled, it has limitations. Firstly, as a source of inspiration and influence, it appeals to only a portion of a population. Right before a big game, world class coaches don't send a well crafted memo to their players. They get into the changing room and deliver powerhouse speeches.

As incredible as an idea can be, the written word is rarely as compelling as when it's delivered personally. If you want to tell someone you love them, you look directly into their eyes and say those three magic words. Out loud. Words simply carry meaning. Conviction is what gives them their true power.

A leader creates clarity from confusion, turns fear into confidence and mobilises people to act in pursuit of a better future. You can't lead your team into battle with an underwhelming whisper.

Those who can articulate the way forward, who inspire with powerful messages, who motivate and provide clarity and make meaning when they speak; these will be the leaders of the near future. Your ability to step up and cut through the noise of mass media, to provoke new insights, to challenge the status quo and bring every group you speak to closer to the central vision of your organisation is what will set you apart.

You've got to get good, really good, at speakership. Sharing your voice to larger and larger groups.

You've got to get rockstar good at spreading messages that matter. Sharing your ideas with the world.

The notion that you influence those around you with the quality of your ideas and the conviction with which you deliver them is not new. History is steeped in the rallying cries of great men and women who have stood up and led—out loud—and in doing so brought others together to build movements and campaigns that have quite literally changed the world.

As we write this, the most popular TED talk of all time—Sir Ken Robinson's treatise on schools killing creativity in children—has been viewed 32 million times, and not always just by a single person at their PC. It's been shown in groups, classrooms, conferences and more. Consider the impact that twenty minute presentation has had around the globe.

Think of the number of lives that will be different (and *better*) as a result of that meme being powerfully shared with educators the world over. This is a shining example of speakership. If the *only* thing Sir Ken did in his life was deliver that speech, he would have had more impact on the world than 99% of all people that have ever lived.

Now more than ever, we need inspired leaders who inspire us. Challenging leaders who challenge us. Now more than ever, speakership *is* leadership.

In business and in life, mastery of speakership creates opportunity and impact. Those willing to invest the time and effort into developing their speakership skills will inevitability find themselves with more opportunities, more invitations, and the growing confidence to take those opportunities in both hands. There isn't a personal development program in the world that will accelerate your leadership growth more than committing to standing on a stage, or at the front of the meeting room, and auditioning to lead. Speakership is leadership, and every tribe needs a leader. Will it be you?

Speakership is leadership

Humans are tribal and no tribe exists without a chief. People naturally gather themselves into groups and demand to be led. Leadership is so vital to human nature that a tribe without a formal chief will create one, appointing the best credentialed person to the position—whether they like it or not. Similarly, a leader without a tribe will *create* a tribe. A single person with a powerful idea and the speakership skills to share it effectively will inevitably rally a group of like-minded individuals around them, and so a movement is created.

Some leadership theorists have identified innate traits within people that lend themselves to leadership, but research consistently reveals that our most powerful leaders are often found in the most unlikely places. They have often overcome hardships and distinct disadvantages to get there. Anyone can develop their leadership capability and learn ways to be more effective and influential just as anyone can learn to swim, or speak Spanish.

There are three critical components of leadership that all leadership theories share. It doesn't matter whether you're a servant leader, a transformational leader, an authentic leader, an autocrat, or a dictator. You might subscribe to management by wandering around, total quality management, just in time leadership, flattened pyramids, distributed leadership, or leadership as enquiry. It doesn't matter. All models share these three ideas:

Leaders create clarity from confusion

Leaders point the way, shape the vision and light the path. It's your job to articulate what needs to be done. Most people turn up to work wanting to do a great job. Unfortunately, in many organisations no one can articulate quite what that means. How are you going to create clarity?

Leaders turn fear into confidence

Leaders provide energy and conviction that spreads like an infection through the tribe. Leaders are able to instil within people a confidence that the job can be done, that the team has what it takes. With great leadership, teams will achieve amazing results they thought perhaps weren't possible. How will you inspire confidence?

Leaders mobilise people to take action towards a better future

Leaders inspire people to act. Everybody turns up to work with discretionary energy, that they *could* choose to apply, or not. Great leaders harness every last drop of that energy. They inspire and activate their teams to get up out of their metaphorical seats and get moving.

How can you make this happen?

Those three ideas combine to mean that leadership is leveraged influence. It's about taking the positive impact you could have and multiplying it many times over. One person can't change the world, but a person that inspires a movement certainly can. It is your ability to spread messages that matter. Forget the over-hyped hot-air balloon "rah-rah" speaker with nothing of value to say. For the worthy leader with great ideas that can't get any traction because the audience isn't listening, speakership is the missing link.

7 HALLMARKS OF SPEAKERSHIP

Speakership is leadership. And here's the top 7 reasons it's no longer an extra, it's essential.

1. It's the influence amplifier

October 2001. Steve Jobs and his team at Apple have developed a product that will revolutionize the way the world listens to music. It will go on to disrupt the entire music industry, democratise pre-existing musical hierarchies, and transform the way artists think about hit records. How does a company that has thrown away the rule book promote this product to the opinion leaders and key market players? A high tech video presentation? A multi-media extravaganza?

Apple holds a special event at its headquarters in Cupertino, inviting media and industry pundits. Dressed in his iconic black turtleneck and jeans, Jobs stands in front of the small crowd and speaks.

'A thousand songs in your pocket'.

He talks with the conviction of a man who has seen the future and is waiting for the rest of us to catch up. He shares his passion for music, speaks openly of his love for the product design and the features. No one knew then that the within the first 10 years Apple would sell 350 million ipods. And there were sceptics to be sure. But not many people in the room would have bet against Jobs that day.

Personal is powerful.

The dominance of the internet in our everyday lives and the ubiquity of recording devices (did I really have a great holiday if I haven't posted the photos to prove it?) means that anyone can virtually go almost anywhere. We can watch all our favourite bands perform live from the comfort of our couches. TED talks stream into our bedrooms and boardrooms, and amateur livecam footage takes us right into the action of any world event. Universities are increasingly offering their course content online, and in many cases, for free.

And yet, there's nothing quite like being there. In 2014, the world's leading promoter of music concerts—Live Nation—generated 4.73 billion USD in revenue, an increase of more than 25 % from 2010 levels. Inspirational, educational conferences like TED and South by Southwest are growing. Executive education providers like Harvard and MIT continue to see an average growth rate of 7% with the primary delivery method being face to face.

So why? Why the desire to be in the room?

From concerts to conferencing, there's no filter when you're face to face in a live experience. You get to be in synchronicity with the presenter, or the artist. There's no time delay, no editing, and the potential for human connection is huge. Leadership theorists talk about authentic leadership as being real, honest, and raw. A live event brings those attributes to the fore and enables an audience to feel the power of the personal.

There's life affirming magic in a shared live experience. Wherever more than a few people are gathered there's an energy that is greater than the sum of the individuals in the room. Great presenters, educators, leaders and performers harness this energy to bring transformational experiences.

Our brains are amazing at creating contextual memories. We remember holidays because our senses are overloaded—the sights, the sounds, the new smells. We lock in the feelings of freedom, of happiness and fun. It's the same when we go to concerts and conferences—if we laugh, we learn. If we're moved by a live performance it has a totally different feel to that of watching a great movie. The difference is even noticeable between watching a movie at home, and seeing the same movie in the atmosphere of the cinemas. It's the variation in energy, in emotion and experience. The power of the personal.

Think about watching a sports event live compared to watching it on the big screen at your local sports bar. The chill in the air as the stadium lights take effect, the roar of the crowd as the first big tackle is made. Being there live is unbeatable. Our memory is massively influenced by the strength of our feelings at the time. Relevant, well researched content delivered confidently makes a good speech. It's not a great speech until it's emotionally compelling. Think of the most famous speeches, and the most memorable moments in them. Martin Luther King had an excellent point, to be sure, but would the world have taken the same degree of notice had he not passionately declared "I have a dream!" with such emotion? Even today, watching that speech—and that particular moment when he goes off script and speaks from the heart—makes your skin tingle.

Inspirational leaders take all this experiential knowledge into their working environments, and then turn up in person to speak about what matters most. They don't send memos, or ask Peter in PR to draft a media release. They step up and get face to face with their people.

Getting really good at talking to crowds is not a 'nice to have' extra in your leadership toolkit. It's a fundamental of 21st century leadership. It's a fundamental of *all* leadership.

2. It's exponentially efficient

Developing your mastery of speaking in public, leading out loud, is more than just feel-good motivation for the masses. It's ruthlessly efficient.

Singing off the same song sheet, getting everyone on the same page, realigning the values and vision—it doesn't matter what you call it, there's a sure fire way to ensure everyone in your organisation or team gets the same message. Leverage your influence by bringing everyone together so they can hear the message from the source. Hear it together in congregation so they can truly *feel* the alignment, not just know it.

Mary Barra took over as the CEO of American car giant General Motors in January 2014 right before the company plunged into a safety crisis leading to a massive recall of 2.4 million cars. Car manufacturers have 5 days to notify officials of a potential safety issue even when they don't know what's causing the problem or how to fix it. In the case of the faulty ignition switches on Chevrolet Cobalts, GM took 10 years. Tragically, 13 people died as a direct result of the fault when their cars lost power and they crashed. How could a company that was so big, making so many cars, fail so spectacularly?

Already bailed out to the tune of 50 billion USD in a taxpayer supported bankruptcy, GM had been through five CEOs in the previous six years leading to unparalleled regulatory, governmental and investor scrutiny. Being the first female CEO in the history of the company meant a lot of people were watching closely to see how Barra would handle the company as it lurched from one disaster to the next. Everyone acknowledged that a culture change was needed, but questioned how it could be done. General Motors has 220,000 employees around the world with 30,000 working in product development alone. Someone, somehow, had to get the right hand talking to the left hand, and to the foot soldiers on the factory floor, and to the brains trust at the top of organisation. Someone had to reconnect all these parts back to the heart of the company. That person was Mary Barra.

By April 2014 Barra had testified before a congressional subcommittee, stumped up early to the $35 million maximum fine for the late notification, and met with the grieving families of the victims. Back in Detroit, she assembled 200+ engineers in the cafeteria of one of the plants to instil the new messages around product safety and communication processes.

Barra could have sent a memo. Or a glossy brochure with infographics and flow charts, perhaps a graph or two. A corporate report might have done the trick. Instead she fronted up and had her speech beamed across to world to all employees. A ruthlessly efficient way to ensure that everyone in the company heard the new direction directly from the source.

Two months later, GM held a Global Town Hall meeting where once again Barra addressed the entire 220,000 strong workforce to reinforce the cultural changes she was leading. She released the full report of the independent review conducted by former US Attorney Anton Valukas and said this:

"I can tell you the report is extremely thorough, brutally tough and deeply troubling. For those of us who have dedicated our lives to this company, it is enormously painful to have our shortcomings laid out so vividly. I was deeply saddened and disturbed as I read the report.

"But this isn't about our feelings or our egos. This is about our responsibility to act with integrity, honour and a commitment to excellence.

"With all of our colleagues around the world watching today, I want it known that this recall issue isn't merely an engineering or manufacturing or legal problem, it represents a fundamental failure to meet the basic needs of these customers.

"Our job is clear: To build high quality, safe vehicles. In this case with these vehicles, we didn't do our job. We failed these customers. We must face up to it and learn from it. To that end, on behalf of GM, we pledge that we will use the findings and recommendations from this report as a template for strengthening our company."

By choosing to stand up and speak directly to her entire work-force Barra leveraged the power of her lone voice. She was able to efficiently cut through the typical noise of business and communicate with a clear honest signal. No ambiguity, no reading between the lines of another long, boring, corporate memo. By speaking directly to the challenges, reiterating the driving values behind the organisation, and painting a clear picture of the next steps to take, Mary Barra leveraged her influence. Not like the slide deck touting, memo sending, excuse making, responsibility avoiding, poor excuses for leaders that are around today. She demonstrated speakership at its absolute finest, and leadership as it's meant to be. These are the people we wish to work for.

3. It's the ultimate personal development vehicle

Leadership development programs are big news and big business. It's universally acknowledged that leadership training and development is important, an investment critical to achieving business goals and expanding the capabilities of those on their way to the top. In the US alone, the leadership development industry is worth $14 billion per annum. Every year thousands of employees embark on leadership training designed to promote and encourage the mindset and skills necessary to lead. All the Ivy League Universities run comprehensive programs pitched at different levels of expertise and experience.

What are some of the fundamentals of this type of training?

There's plenty of knowledge acquisition around finance, strategy, global marketing, change, innovation, corporate responsibility, marketing, data analytics and the like. To be effective in the international marketplace this level of thinking is simply the price of entry into the game. In fact, a number of the programs insist that candidates prepare for leadership programs by completing post-graduate equivalent study in topics such as accounting, commercial law and finance before they travel to the campus to begin their leadership intensive.

Once leadership development begins in earnest the topics include self-awareness, leadership styles and personality profiling. The emphasis shifts from knowing facts, knowing how and when to apply theoretical frameworks, to knowing yourself. Why?

Because arguably the very first and most important person you'll ever lead is yourself. The reason self-discipline, integrity and character are rated so highly by followers is that no-one likes being asked to do something by someone who isn't already doing it themselves. If you can't figure out who you are and what makes you tick you haven't got a hope of understanding how best to influence and inspire others.

If you don't know how to regulate your own personal state of mind, what is the chance you'll be able to help others to do something extraordinary?

Developing self-awareness is a hugely important part of any leader's journey. Understanding our own psychological make-up and exploring our emotional triggers and vulnerabilities enables us to master our personal weaknesses, or at least make peace with them, and then set about leading others in an authentic way.

If you want to better know yourself and understand how you respond under pressure, give a public talk. Speaking in public is the ultimate personal development vehicle. It's a crucible of self-discovery.

There is something phenomenally challenging about speaking in public. Everyone is looking at you, and waiting. Waiting for you to speak. There is nowhere for you to hide. If you want to accelerate your leadership development, and get really comfortable in your own skin no matter how many people are watching and waiting, put your hand up to speak in public more often.

Many leadership intensives for emerging leaders involve presentations where participants are invited (compelled!) to give a five to ten minute presentation about something that has moved them, or something they've learned. You'd think it was an easy assignment. Only 300 seconds to fill. No additional research needed. Each speaker is literally *the* subject matter expert on the topic. The speaker can't be wrong, is in total control of what they share, and nothing is at stake. It's not reality TV, no one gets voted off or sent home.

And yet, some participants totally freak out. They don't sleep the night before, their bodies show physical signs of distress—elevated heart rate, sweaty palms, and dry mouths. This is where the work is done. Precious metal is refined under intense heat. The impurities melt away, leaving the pure, raw, and extremely valuable material behind. It's the same process when you step up to speak out. The exposure is what does the trick. It strips away any artifice, pretence or posturing. Even for those speakers who are in command of their nerves, the experience is often enlightening.

Whether there's a transaction in a commercial sense or not, in every interaction people are buying from each other. Buying into ideas. Buying into causes. Buying into tribes. But people don't buy ideas for rational reasons. They might justify it later that way, but the initial decision is driven emotionally. They buy you. They buy your reasons for saying what you're saying. They buy your conviction around what you're saying. In a sense, when you audition to lead by speaking in public, they buy who you are.

People very quickly form judgements about who you are and what you are saying. The more you develop your sense of self, the better you'll become at speaking to groups. The more you speak to groups, the stronger your sense of self will become. Your leadership capability is expanded every time you put yourself out there. It's not easy. Your flaws are exposed, you're at peak vulnerability. But that's how the growing gets done.

George Mitchell is one of the world's most respected peace negotiators. President Bill Clinton's Special Envoy to Northern Ireland from 1995 -2001, he was instrumental in the Good Friday Agreement of 1998. He's served as a director on the boards of The Walt Disney Company, Federal Express, Xerox and the Boston Red Sox and now—an octogenarian—he regularly gives speeches all over the globe. Mitchell is not a natural extrovert, and had a reputation for being mild-mannered and cerebral. Asked by Harvard Business Review how he became such a successful public figure despite this reputation, he said:

> "When I ran for governor and lost, that was the description of me. I read and heard so much of it that I came to believe it. I thought I'd never again be involved in politics and certainly couldn't possibly win an election. But you learn from your mistakes and improve your performance. I don't know how many thousands of speeches I've given, but every time, I try to do the best I can and hope it's better than the

one before. In politics, when you make a mistake, it's on the front page, so you become clearly aware of your faults and work at it more."

4. It's the certainty filter

If you spend too much time in your own head there's a risk that you're avoiding the litmus test of certainty. New concepts and 3am ideas that sound fabulous in your head and seem like self-evident truths can sound false as soon as they've escaped from your mouth.

One of the reasons speakership is such an important aspect of your ability and capability to lead is that you force yourself to verbalise what you stand for, what you believe, and what you think the next best steps are for everyone in the room. Publicly owning your thoughts by declaring them forces a deeper level of thought. Having to stringently prepare this thought for scrutiny by an audience calls on the courage of your convictions. No more the sanctuary of introspection!

Our understanding of how speech operates is changing. The dominant model of how speech works is that we have conscious thoughts of what we want to say and then we plan it, preparing in advance of the verbalisation. But how often do we say things we don't mean? Or rather we thought we meant it until we heard it? We hear our own opinion vocalised and instantly we want to adapt it, clarify it or dismiss it altogether. "That's not what I meant." This is not just a question of our ability to articulate our thoughts. Our thoughts actually change once we've heard them out loud. It's the certainty filter in action.

Some researchers now think that our speech is not entirely planned and that one way we know what we are saying is to hear what we've said.

The challenge for introverted leaders is to allow all the great thoughts and ideas out of your head and through speech release them into the room. This enables you to solidify or modify your viewpoint based on what you hear yourself say. If you are on the introverted side of the spectrum you can think of it as 'thinking out loud'. People will see you as a more open and approachable leader. Speak even when you are not 100% clear and if artfully done the people that work with you will gain a sense of ownership around your ideas. They get to participate in the journey of getting to 'certain'.

Don't sit in the dark alone, solving the problems of the world only to announce that you (alone) have fixed the problem, declaring 'I have the answer!' Instead speak as you go, let them know what you are thinking along the way and they will go further with you than you could ever imagine. The old saying "if you want to go fast, go alone; but if you want to go far, go together" talks to this ideal.

For extroverts, the risk is that all your 'reckons' get equal air-time without the requisite internal filtering. This can be confusing for everyone around you, and cause people to tune out as they may judge your words to be careless or unrefined. Extroverts really need to think before they speak. Musings need to be framed as such and quarantined accordingly.

Many extroverts trust their well-honed swagger to pull them through at live events. They are often found presenting with a minimum of preparation and maximum audience connection. At some point in a leader's career this energetic reliance is not enough. The leader gets marginalised, passed over, relegated to a people or partners role but never getting a seat at the big table. They don't get taken seriously for their thinking, for their ideas.

Speaking regularly in front of groups of people; your colleagues, staff, and total strangers, provides a fantastic opportunity to get certainty about what you really think. It helps you create clarity for yourself and deliver that clarity to those you aspire to lead. Extroverts need to plan to think before they speak and introverts need to think out loud.

5. It's the opinion shifter

The legacy of inspirational orators is evident throughout the last few centuries. We immediately think of Winston Churchill, William Wilberforce, and Martin Luther King as examples of people who changed the course of world events and human rights through their ability to influence and inspire others to take courageous action. And crucially, their influence extended to helping others change their minds.

Oprah Winfrey calls these times of transformation 'aha' moments. The realisation that there is a new way to view a problem, or a situation. The acknowledgement that what we previously thought to be correct and true may in fact be false. John Newton, composer of Amazing Grace penned the famous lyric 'I once was lost, but now I'm found, was blind, but now I see'. People aren't predisposed to having their minds changed at any given moment. You only needs to spend a minute or two browsing the comment thread of a contentious news article online to know that most people's minds are thoroughly made up, and are in no state to be un-made the vast majority of the time.

The Kings and the Wilberforces of history were influential not only because they spoke so powerfully to their own tribe of believers but because they espoused a new future that enabled those outside of the 'already convinced' to change their minds. They spoke with impact and influence, with conviction but also empathy. They provided the motivation people needed to critically analyse their opinions, and *then* the convincing argument required to shift them. Delivering the latter without the former is about as effective as bare-knuckle punching an armoured car.

How essential is this skill—the ability to shift opinion—in modern leadership?

The ability to speak with a group of employees, stakeholders, media commentators, or investors and help them all see a situation or problem in a new light is a fundamental of 21st century leadership. In a contemporary context it's easy to underestimate the transformational aspect of great speakers addressing issues that matter. We can access so much information from so many different sources, why should one person's ten minute talk hold such great sway? What is it about the speaker/listener experience that lays the foundation for a paradigm shift, a new way of thinking, or a change of heart?

Courage is contagious.

It takes a moment of inspiration to speak out against the status quo. Leaders are often in the position of putting their necks on the line for a new initiative, or taking the heat for a bruising restructure. The personal conviction that's required to stand at the front and deliver the clarion call acts as a catalyst for others to be both contemplative and brave. The sharing of a personal story or a personal truth galvanizes the listeners to dig deeper into their own reserves of courage and commitment. Standing up for what you believe in is bold and daring. It makes you vulnerable. And when you do, it breathes a little life into those listening; it lifts and elevates their perspectives and shifts their consciousness. Your words stoke the embers of belief within the listeners and they are inspired to line up behind you as their leader. Isn't that what we need more of in our organizations? Leaders who influence others to take a fresh look at opportunities and challenges, and ultimately mobilise others to take action for a better future.

6. It's the learning accelerator

Speakership is the new media whose origins are very firmly rooted in the past. From the old sages of Ancient Greek, to the Romans, to the Prophets of Eastern Mysticism and the revolutionary preachers of the Reformation, our civilisation is built on a longstanding tradition of great leaders making speeches to influence and inspire. Back then, speakers faced enormous difficulties bringing their messages to the masses, sometimes giving hundreds of public addresses every year.

There were no printing presses, and even when technology allowed greater distribution of the written word, access was strictly controlled by the powerful elite.

As technology changed so did communication methods. Think of those endearing old photos of families huddled around the wireless to hear the great speeches of Churchill and King George VI. Originally all the speeches had to be broadcast live, there was no capability for recording, editing and finessing. While it wasn't perfect, it was real. And in the case of the stuttering King George VI, the vulnerability led to an authentic bond with his people during the darkest days of World War II.

But then it all changed. The rise of marketing and PR in the commercial sphere meant that 'truth' was massaged into its most palatable form. Business leaders and politicians quickly became adept of the art of the soundbite but even so, it became increasingly difficult for them to manage their messages. Everything they said was filtered through someone else's lens before reaching its intended audience.

And then it all changed, again! The internet enables both the sender and receiver of the message to take control of their content. No more intermediaries, no more unwanted editorial interference. As consumers of ideas we can seek out information anytime we like and go directly to the source. Thought leaders, business leaders, opinion shapers, thinkers, and academics all tweet, write blogs, post photos to Facebook and Instagram and, most powerfully of all, share videos of themselves speaking. Unfiltered and unfettered; we chose who, when and where we want to watch.

Hearing and seeing someone speak, even when recorded, is like mainlining their heart and mind directly to yours. What this new media lacks in terms of a live spine-tingling experience is made up by convenience and accessibility. If you can't get to TED in person you can get there virtually.

And for those who want to lead and inspire others, to spread messages that matter, you can now have ultimate control of your content and disseminate it widely. Business leaders like Mary Barra are able to transmit their speeches directly to their huge teams without any obstruction.

You don't have to dumb down your message into tiny soundbites to suit the mass media, you can *smarten down* your message by speaking authentically, directly to your audience, your tribe. Even better, the audience can now pass the message on in its entirety. Email and social media distribution mean that a presentation which influences one person will often be forwarded to a hundred more.

Movements like the Khan Academy demonstrate these new possibilities perfectly. Salman Khan was unable to continue tutoring his brother's children in mathematics when they moved to another state. Not content to let them flounder, he recorded videos explaining the mathematical concepts to them and shared them on YouTube. They became an international phenomenon. Children all over the world started watching his videos to improve their mathematical skills.

His project, which began as a favour to his relatives and has grown into a legitimate multi-national teaching organisation, made such an impact on learning that it started an educational revolution—the 'flipped classroom'. Some institutions are now providing all their classwork and lectures as videos to be watched at home, while the homework is performed in class with the help of the teachers.

Live learning, with its opportunity for immediate feedback and contemporaneous discussion, will always have a place. As authors, we are firmly committed to the idea of making the teaching and learning aspects of your leadership a live, physical multi-sensory experience whenever you can. The future will require you to also be able to apply the principles of speakership virtually and asynchronously. Learning is accelerated when you get your messages to more people, more often, through media that you control.

The ubiquitous impact of the internet means that your audience can listen when they are ready, at their convenience, when their hearts and minds are receptive and open. Never before has there been a more powerful, influential leadership platform.

It's just like the old days. Only better.

7. It's the curator of culture

Speakership creates and curates culture.

In the post-industrial age, hierarchical authoritarian leadership styles are being forced to make way for those that create empowered employees with flat organisation charts. Little attention is paid to length of service and almost none to the old fashioned idea of working your way slowly to the top.

For many organisations engaged in the war for talent their competitive advantage lies in their culture. They've created work worth doing, and cultures worth belonging to. The mistake some onlookers make is to copy and paste the trappings of culture without searching for the deeper meaning that underpins the shiny baubles.

Take a look at Google or any of the major tech companies and you see beautiful campuses with exotic kitchens pumping out every type of food imaginable, and of course a ping pong table with connecting slide to the floor below. "I know", declares the misguided imitator, "we'll get a play area, and an in-house cafeteria, and all our cultural challenges will be solved".

Except of course, these tangible expressions of culture aren't a culture in-and-of themselves. The cafeterias and the ping pong tables didn't create the culture at Google, the culture at Google created them. And what created the culture at Google? Leadership. Real, authentic, human leadership.

There's no such thing as a corporate entity. You can't ring up and ask to speak to Telstra. Or Qantas. Or Starbucks. There's no such thing as organisational culture. The organisation doesn't exist separate from its people in any meaningful sense. When you hear people speak about organisational culture they're really talking about how things get done around here, by the people who work here.

And who declares that vision? Who establishes how it's going to be in your company, in your workplace?

It's the leader. The leader gives life to the culture of an organisation by articulating the vision of the tribe. The words chosen by the leader send very clear messages to the entire team about what matters most around here and how things get done. Speakership creates culture.

Steve Jobs was described as having a reality distortion field around him. He demanded excellence and refused to accept that some things were technically impossible. Cynics called him crazy, and yet his teams developed products that would not or could not have been conceived anywhere else. He gave voice to possibility and spoke the future into being.

Leaders create culture by conceiving, nurturing and articulating vision—the big *why*—every time they speak. You can have fancy logos and slogans designed and pasted onto your office walls but when you get in front of your troops, it's you who sets the cultural tone. Your talk determines their walk.

Great leaders are also great listeners. Noticing the intangible aspects of what makes your company worth working for, the cultural capital of the people who work there, and articulating this back to your teams is the art of cultural curation. Observing the creativity, the genius, the problem solving and the otherwise unseen work that goes on and streamlining that into a coherent set of values or ideas is cultural curation.

Speakership curates culture.

In the war for talent, it's not the ping pong table that will set you and your organisation apart. It's the ability you have to bring your vision to life. Your ability to create and reflect through the power of your spoken word, a culture that people want to be part of, doing work that's worth doing.

And here's a leadership challenge for you. Go back over the last few speeches you've given, the previous meetings you've run, the small group conversations you've had. Have you led through your talk? Have you given voice to the standards, the values, the essence of your culture? Have you languaged what's most important to your company in a way that inspires those around you?

GREAT EXPECTATIONS

Perhaps you're a Senior Leader called on to rev-up the troops, and the thought fills you with dread? Are you having trouble presenting to the board of directors? You might be a middle manager attempting to influence those above and below you in your organisation. Maybe you're just starting out in your career and wondering how to get any-one to listen to your ideas in meetings, or take you seriously when you present new initiatives?

This is not a book designed to help you speak in public without throwing up or succumbing to a panic attack. Though if you think that's a real possibility for you, we still recommend the development strategy detailed in this book. Because so many people fear speaking in public, many so-called experts tend to focus on simply surviving the experience. Filled with unhelpful tricks ("think of the audience naked") and old and outdated modes of content delivery ("tell them what you're going to tell them, tell them, and then tell them what you've told them!"), this type of advice is spectacularly useless. Being confident in your message and standing in the conviction of doing what you know to be the right thing will have a far greater impact on your speaking ability than a trick to distract you from the reality of your situation.

We have a fundamental belief that there is vital connection between the speeches, presentations and talks you give, and effective leadership. It doesn't matter if you're in the boardroom speaking to 12 or the ballroom speaking to 2000, every time you speak you have the opportunity to lead. In a society where every tribe needs a chief, every time you speak you have an *obligation* to lead. Your ability to share messages that matter in a compelling and influential way is a critical leadership capability. It's the new leadership imperative. With this book, our goal is to elevate speakers, to open your eyes to what you're truly capable of (it's extraordinary), and to raise consciousness on the planet by helping people—indeed, by helping you—fulfil your leadership potential.

Do you have any idea how good you can be? You may find it surprising, but our expectations for your improvement are probably much greater than yours.

Yes, we believe your potential as a speaker and leader is far greater than you realise. How can we say that? How could we, not knowing who you are, what experience you have, what natural aptitude you possess, how could we possibly have a better sense of your potential than you do? How can we know, without having met you, what you're capable of?

Strictly speaking, we can't. Out of the thousands and thousands of people that will read this book we don't know who will take up the challenge and become truly world class. But we do know this: most people have no idea how good they can be. Most people have no idea how much better they can become. And most people are afraid to really be all that they can be. The problem with potential is that it's something unrealised. By the very definition of the word, it's latent.

You've seen presentations, speeches and motivational talks that blew you away. Whether in person, or on film, you've been moved by powerful, eloquent, elegant speeches delivered by master communicators. You've probably wished that your boss or coach could be as inspirational as the great leaders and coaches in the movies.

The trouble is, this act of genius can create a barrier. You hear the amazing content and see the dynamic delivery and you may feel as though you could never be that good. The gap feels too wide. While most people observe and appreciate the *content* and effect of the presentation, they fail to notice the higher level of abstraction, the *metapresentation*.

The metapresentation is all the stuff that has been deliberately engineered to make that speech or presentation so powerful. It's the relatively simple techniques and strategies which culminate in making a presentation exponentially more influential. It's the stuff that separates amateurs from professionals. The stuff that separates good from great. It's the stuff which, until you're aware of it, seems as intangible as magic. Arthur C Clarke famously said "Any sufficiently advanced technology is indistinguishable from magic". You can't see what you can't see.

This book will open your eyes to that bigger picture, the overarching framework that enables you to close the gap between where you are now, and what's possible. We hope to make you aware of a whole series of techniques and strategies that will massively improve the power of your speeches. We hope to create a dissonance between what you are currently capable of, and what you will soon come to realise is within your reach.

This dissonance is uncomfortable, but it propels you towards mastery orders of magnitude faster than traditional step by step methods. We will show you the science of influence through the art of oration.

We can't guarantee that the very next time you speak after reading this book, you'll be perfect. But you will have a heightened awareness that raises your expectations of both how well you could speak, and the difference this would make in your workplace, in your team, in your career. It won't be easy, and it requires courage, but the rewards are extraordinary.

You probably already know that there are two ways to enjoy a magic show. The first is to suspend disbelief, to sit in the audience and be amazed when the elephant disappears, or the beautiful assistant is sliced in half, or the magician steps off the platform and hovers in mid-air. It's an enjoyable way to spend an evening, to be treated to an exciting and entertaining show.

The second way to enjoy a magic show is quite the opposite, and rarely do the two kinds of people like to sit next to each other while the show is on! These folks try to deconstruct every illusion, to try to understand what's *really* going on. This kind of observer spends the night craning their head this way and that, trying to spy the mirror, or the false floor, avoiding the distraction of the magician's pure white glove to spy the man in the black outfit in darkness behind.

We're going to take you behind the curtain, show you how the magic of speakership is performed, and shorten your journey to mastery by years. Of course, once you have chosen to try to learn the ways of the magician, you can't turn back. Once you've peeked behind the curtain and learned the secrets, you can't unlearn or forget them later. It's a one way ticket, and once you're committed to that knowledge, you're committed for life.

Once you understand the elements of masterful presentation skills, you will never be able to just 'sit in the audience' again. Every speaker you see, every presentation you witness, every training session, every pep talk, every storytelling session, and every concert; your awareness of presentation skills will pervade every one. You will notice everything a speaker does, what works, and what they could improve. You will have a constant critical commentary running in your head as you observe them speak.

You'll get to the point where watching others speak becomes a little annoying. You'll constantly be aware of the ways that they could improve, things they could do to sharpen the message, or deliver it with more impact, or engage with the audience more deeply. And while it's annoying, it's an important component of your journey to mastery. It *needs* to be this way, in order for you to truly bring the best of yourself to stage when you present.

As an aspiring speaker yourself you'll know how much courage it takes to stand on stage and speak, so your critical mindset ought to be offset with compassion. If you think another speaker is pretty average, you don't have to let your face tell them. The purpose of a critical mindset is to allow you to learn and grow as a speaker, not to bring anyone else down.

Buddha said "Love is the recognition of yourself in another, and delight in the discovery". When you begin to recognise yourself in great presentations and inspiring speeches, you'll know that mastery is within your grasp. You'll have developed the awareness of what you need to improve in order to get to that point.

It's important to know that this mastery of speakership is a skill, and can be developed. The 'magic' that good speakers display isn't innate. They've learnt it. The gap between yourself and an incredible speaker you presently admire is not big because of a difference in talent. It's big because of a difference in timeline. They've already learnt the skills to perform the magic.

Shifting gears

In the chapter after this short piece, we will begin unpacking the nine principles that map the path of your journey as a leader, harnessing and leveraging the capabilities of speakership. For ease of reading, throughout the book we will generally discuss the application of these principles in a large audience format like a conference. However, it's worth spending some time in this chapter highlighting the ways that these skills matter right across the organisation, demonstrating the fact that the tenets of speakership continue to apply far from the spotlight and stage.

For this to work you may have to shift gears as a leader. You may have to mix up how you run team meetings, how you present at the annual conference and the quality of the thinking behind your memos, emails and (shudder!) slide decks.

Using the nine principles in this book, you will run better meetings, coach members of your team more effectively, and negotiate more persuasively. We think your leadership in general will be positively affected by the speakership curriculum... but only if you put it into action.

And while we have your attention on this wider idea of organisational influence, we think that the way most organisations communicate internally is fatally flawed. We think it's a broken element in the business culture of many organisations, and it's something we hope to address. This book contributes to our crusade, seeking to create leaders who are less boring, more impactful, and mindful of the difference they make when they stop managing (simply informing) and start leading (inspiring us all).

We have been thinking a lot about meetings; how much time we waste in them and how bad we are at running them. From the small meetings over a coffee, where mentors offer advice; to the large meetings we call conferences, where leaders inspire and motivate.

We meet to create joint ventures, negotiate deals or simply to get things done. There are plenty of really good reasons to meet, plenty of opportunities to collaborate productively. Why do so few meetings live up to their potential?

We are, collectively, really bad at meetings. Could we turn them around? Could we take them from time wasters to extraordinary agents of change?

If you ask any executive leading a large organisation, they will tell you that huge swathes of their time are taken up in poorly run meetings that suck time and cause extraordinary opportunity loss. In an era when our time is probably one of the top three resources we have, we are squandering it in ineffectual collaborations that drain motivation and productivity.

We reckon enough time and energy has been wasted. It's time to shift gears. As a leader, you have some decisions to make.

You can continue complaining that meetings are a waste of time, or start doing the work to make them powerful agents for change. You can continue to accept a culture that allows BCC and group emails to be substitutes for communicating, or agitate for real, human connection. You can subject your direct reports to "Death by Powerpoint", or inspire and inform with humour and drama next time you speak. You know where we stand. It's time for you to shift gears as a leader. Shift into speakership.

Speakership was developed as part of an extension to the curriculum of Thought Leaders Global. Thought Leaders Global is a leadership development organisation that exists to help clever people be commercially smart. For many years, we've been championing the idea that leaders will be more influential in their business if they balance their *tell, show, ask* ratio.

At times you need to influence people by *telling* them what you would like them to do, at other times you need to *show* them what to do and often you need to *ask* them questions and lead them to discover their own answers, creating their own accountability towards action as a result.

The masterful motivational leader in the business context has six primary modes of influence, each of these modes address primary goals or expectations that the business places on those in charge.

TELL

Leadership speaking *Tell us where we are going*

Strategic authoring *Describe how we will get there*

SHOW

Expertise mentoring *Show us how to lead this shift*

Capability training *Help us get prepared*

ASK

Confidence coaching *Ensure we believe in ourselves*

Solution facilitation *Align all players on the team*

Clearly, this book's primary focus is helping you become rock-star good at leadership speaking, but the speakership principles you're about to learn apply right through these six critical delivery modes.

Sometimes you are in a meeting with one person, sometimes it's a presentation to the board. An offsite leadership retreat with your direct reports requires a different application of the following

9 principles of influence than a 30 minute presentation at your key clients' annual conference. A strategy proposal document includes no speaking at all, but the ideas you present will be vastly more compelling when you apply principles 1 and 2 to their creation.

At heart, this book is about communication, and whether it's in the cafeteria, the training room, the boardroom, or the ballroom; these 9 principles will increase your effectiveness as a leader and help you make a bigger difference across all the projects you touch, and the tribe you serve.

FIX NERVOUS WITH SERVICE

We've heard it claimed that 80% of people are more afraid of speaking than they are of dying. Which means that if they're going to attend a funeral, they're rather do so as the person in the casket than as the one delivering the eulogy! While the science behind this claim is dubious there's no doubt that most people get nervous before they speak in front of a group.

There's a whole industry built around overcoming this nervousness. There are already many great books that focus on how you can overcome your fear of public speaking. Our aspirations for you are much greater than that.

This book is a treatise on speaking as a key leadership imperative.

Our goal is to help guide you along a transformational leadership journey to increase your speakership skills. The greater range of skills you're going to learn in sharing messages that matter will be all the assistance you need to speak without being paralysed by nerves.

It's all about focus.

The first layer of focus is the speaker (*I, me*). The effect this is going to have on your nervous tension is probably pretty obvious. If you make yourself the centre of your focus of attention, you can fall into the trap of over-analysing yourself, and worrying too much about what others might think of you. Unhealthy and unhelpful thoughts—"I'm not good enough. Why should people listen to me? I'm not sure about this"—are the result of a self-centred focus.

The next layer of focus is the audience (*you, them*). This can also be a source of a great deal of nervous tension, as you notice every movement your audience makes, every cough and disinterested expression on their faces. "Are they listening to me? Do they agree with what I'm saying? Why didn't they laugh at that joke?" Many speaking coaches will employ methods of distraction to help a speaker who is stuck in this focus of attention. Strategies like "Imagine the audience is naked", or "Focus on a point floating above their heads" are tricks designed to distract the speaker away from what is capturing the full focus of their attention—the large crowd of people assembled before them.

These tricks are not beneficial. They are treatment of a symptom, not the cause, and as such even when they work, they only work so long as the speaker remembers to keep distracting themselves. As soon as they lose control of that attention… the nervousness and all the stress associated with it comes flooding back.

Even the more healthy versions of audience focus aren't that helpful. For example, seeking out the 'smilers', or focusing only on those people in the room who are engaged and present and giving 'good face' might mean you end up delivering your message tailored only to a small percentage of the room. Even worse, you may distort your message in an effort to be popular, at the expense of actually making the important point that you came to present.

The key to controlling nervous tension is to rise to the highest layer of focus—that of the tribe (*we, us*). This focus of attention is one that is inclusive not just of everyone in the room but everyone involved; whether sitting in the front row, the back row, or not even in attendance at all. You're speaking for everyone that your ideas impact, wherever they may be in the world.

This focus of attention helps to put you in a mindset of service. It forces you to think about what the room and the wider tribe need to hear. This is a fast-track method of getting over yourself and delivering the difference in the world that you were born to make. It helps you speak with clarity, it helps you speak with conviction, and it helps ensure that your presentation is structured in a way that elevates the message you're spreading in service of the tribe to which you belong.

A person speaking from this focus doesn't have the need to worry about their credentials, or what some particular member of the audience is thinking. A leader speaking with this focus can deliver their message with conviction; unconcerned by their fears or insecurities, undistracted by anything about the room or the lead up that hasn't been ideal; and instead concentrate purely on the impact of their message and its influence on the tribe.

A presentation *for the tribe* changes the state of the room.

The form of the speech is more of a conversation than a presentation. The majority of the information is going one way, but great empathy for the audience and a concerted effort to keep the focus of attention on the tribe, helps make it *feel* like a conversation for those in the audience. Their minds are encouraged to think and silently contribute to the discussion you're leading. It's engagement in the true sense of the word.

Ready to take the step up? To go behind the curtain and learn the key skills for becoming an inspirational leader — one who talks the walk?

Let's go.

THE SPEAKERSHIP MODEL

It's late on a Sunday night and your phone rings. You're annoyed, but when the caller ID reveals 'John – CEO' you arrange your face and swipe to answer. "Okay, no problem John. 45 minutes? No, no that'll be fine. Leave it with me. Inspiring? Entertaining? No problem. Thanks John". And just like that you have 48 hours to prepare a keynote address for your annual sales conference. The pre-booked professional speaker can't make it, and your CEO John has selected you as the replacement. 300 staff, some of whom you've met, some of whom even like you. What are you going to do?

This model codifies the evolution that a speaker takes from beginner to expert. From student to superstar. It takes the three expanding points of focus, and shows you *who* they can be focused on, *what* you must do at the level of focus, and *why* that's going to be important.

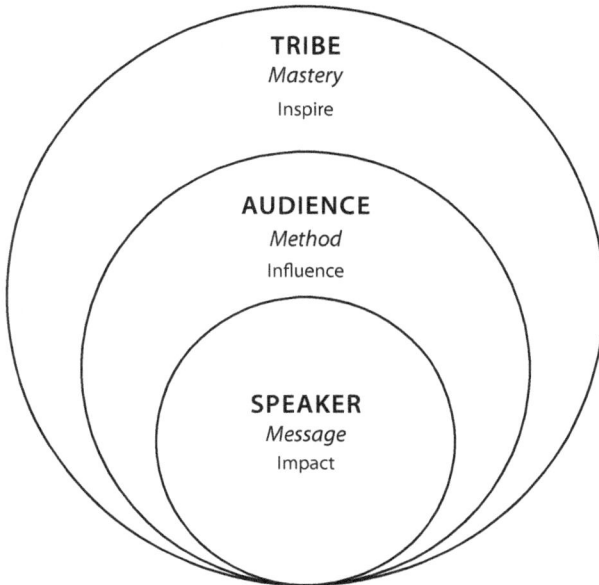

TRIBE
Mastery
Inspire

AUDIENCE
Method
Influence

SPEAKER
Message
Impact

Focus

You'll recognise the three layers of focus—Speaker, Audience, Tribe—from the previous discussion of nervous tension. We've already spoken about how great speakers manage to engage the whole room in a conversation, and generate a feeling of purpose and togetherness with the tribe. When you speak, you need to pay attention, but not just to what is going on inside or even around you. The key difference between those who are good on stage and those who are truly world class is that they pay attention to different things, or more accurately, to additional things.

The expert speakers still know what's going on inside and around them, but they have lifted their attention to a higher place. They are watching the dance between them and the audience; they have a part of their attention on their own content and a continuous flexibility around how they are weaving the whole experience together.

They move seamlessly between a self-awareness (do I need to speed up, slow down, change slides?) to an awareness of the audience in the room (they're laughing, they're leaning forwards) to an awareness of what's actually going on for the entire room and wider tribe that needs to be addressed (is this message getting through, is this audience engaged enough to take action?). Focusing on the tribe—on the collective interests of everyone who will be impacted by your speech—is the best way to get yourself out of your own way and into the service of the room. It helps you address that which truly matters; outcomes.

Notice that each layer of the model does not replace those below it. A speaker must always retain some awareness of self, for example, even when they're endeavouring not to make themselves the focus of the presentation. When you think about your role as a speaker you have to tick off a basic checklist of self-focused items as entry level to the game: personal appearance, hygiene, personal style, professionalism, and preparation. It's not wrong to focus on yourself, it's just not helpful to stay with that as your sole focus.

As you lift your attention from the bottom layer to the top, you maintain your connection to those below. When your attention is up, and in service of the tribe, you will naturally bring the best version of yourself to the fore. Your passion is unleashed, your conviction exposed for all to see. The audience will be treated to an authentic and compelling speech from a real human being, a person they may agree or disagree with, but whom they will respect. When your focus is on the service of the tribe; when you strip away pretence and pride, self-interest and doubt; that's when the audience is exposed to inspirational leadership that mobilises them to action. That's speakership.

Capability

Just as there are three layers of focus, there are three capabilities you need to truly master the art of speakership. Anyone who aspires to leadership has to develop command and control of their *message* and *method* to reach speakership *mastery*. This is where the bulk of the preparatory work is done. The tools, techniques and strategies for climbing the ladder to mastery compose much of the rest of this book. Here's the high level overview.

Message

Message describes the information you're sharing with the world, not just the value of the message, but the elegance with which it is constructed and described. The greatest idea on earth is of no value to anyone if no-one understands or remembers it. A truly powerful message is carefully designed so it can be digested easily and understood by people with a full spectrum of life experiences, motivations, and learning styles.

A truly powerful message is one that is illustrated beautifully with models and metaphors, woven into compelling stories, and supported by empirical evidence. A truly powerful message can be learned quickly by the audience and shared, creating a meme with lasting impact.

Method

The way you deliver your message is the method. This encompasses your skill in delivering your content with flair and purpose. It means you use humour, movement, stories, characters and drama to deliver your message in a manner that increases audience engagement and information retention.

Method means having all the tools and techniques to capture and maintain the attention of an audience, and deliver the message in an entertaining and memorable fashion. Beyond simple party tricks, or the indefinable personality trait 'charisma', nailing method means knowing when and how to use any and all of these tools and techniques to influence the audience and deliver the message.

Mastery

Of the three capabilities, mastery is the most intangible. It describes the ability of a world-class presenter to control their focus and awareness to serve the room. Mastery is the 'third eye' speakers use to gauge the collective emotional state of the audience, and their response to the presentation as it's being delivered. Speakers in mastery describe having an almost out-of-body experience, in that they can see themselves on the stage delivering the talk while also being aware of the changes they'll need to make to both their message and their method on the fly to better meet the needs of both the audience and the wider tribe.

It's a little like the intuition that is born from experience. Think of the way a world class tennis player can read subtle cues from their opposition and make adjustments to their swing without even being conscious of noticing the cue in the first place. That's not possible when you're a beginner and your mind is flooded with thoughts of grip, swing, foot movement, shot selection and strategy. Like winning Wimbledon, the journey to speakership mastery is not one that will happen overnight. It's a path that takes time to tread, and experiences along the way play an important role in your development.

There will be successes, and inevitably failures, the only certainty being that at some point you will need to speak before you are ready. Comedian Steven Wright once said "Experience is something you don't get until just after you need it", and it's hard to imagine a domain outside of public speaking where that statement rings truer. Mastery is only possible when you are so in control of your message and method you create space in your consciousness for an even greater awareness of what's happening around you.

Outcome

This portion of the model reminds us that at each stage of the speakership journey our efforts create different outcomes. While our purpose is always to serve the audience, the wider tribe, and to deliver value, as we move towards mastery we reap a greater reward and we multiply our contribution. The outcome is absolutely crucial to engaging with your tribe. It provides the reason to take a service-based mindset, it's the source of your passion, and it keeps you motivated in moments of low results.

The outcome usually revolves around pursuing a better future. Whether this is a better environment, a better result for your company, a better technological goal, a better... it all adds up to improving for the future. You need to be exactly clear on *why* you are doing what you're doing, if you want to do it well.

If you don't have a reason that you truly believe in, you have no ability to connect with the audience, and no incentive to thoroughly develop the speakership capabilities.

As you improve your message and method, and use experience to progress through the levels of focus, it's useful to have a reminder of the outcome you're working towards and what's realistic to expect at each stage of your journey. Accelerated growth and rapid progress are both possible. Understanding where you sit in the Speakership model helps you plan your next steps.

Impact

When your focus is on yourself as speaker, you are perfecting your message, getting really clear about what you want to say and starting to polish how you're going to deliver it. You might practise your jokes, rehearse your stories, and particularly focus on having something worthwhile to say. You're crafting messages that matter.

At this first level, you are a speaker with a message hoping to have impact. You want your listeners to know that you are in the room and have something worth listening to. Your presence commands their attention, and they sit up and take notice. Your goal is to land your key points, and for your ideas to have cut-through; to make an impact.

At this first level, audiences both large and small appreciate your professional proficiency and your ability to express your ideas with elegance and ease. You feel the satisfaction of knowing that you've made a difference by giving voice to good ideas and speaking with courage and conviction.

Influence

The next step is to move beyond impact to influence. While an impactful presentation will catch a person's attention, an influential presentation will change a person's thinking. We've all had an experience where we've walked away from a meeting or a presentation with new understanding or insight. Our thinking has shifted, we see our immediate problems and challenges in new lights. That's influence.

When you focus more on your audience, their experience, their doubts and their immediate concerns, you are better able to influence their futures. Using all the methodology of speakership gives you the best opportunity to influence your audience. You've moved beyond the focus on yourself and your message and are now able to shape what's going on in the room.

Influence affects the way your audience will think about your subject in the future. Influence is not about aggressively changing opinions. It's about shaping their ways of thinking. Opinions are in the moment. Ways of thinking stretch forward through time.

Influence means the audience can continue further than the subject material that you have just given them, You set them up with robust, challenging ways of thinking, and they'll be able to continue processing and collecting knowledge on the subject well beyond the short time you spent together.

If you influence your audience to think a certain way about your subject material, you also have the power to influence the way they'll approach other subject material, no matter how distantly linked. The value of this is incredibly high.

As a result of the time you've spent with the audience, whether it's an in-house group or a crowd of strangers, they'll have an expanded sense of what's possible, they might be reconsidering a previously tightly held position, they'll have questions, and they'll be keen to explore the boundaries and implications of their altered thinking.

That's when speakership leads you to thought leadership.

Inspire

This is the ultimate outcome to which speakership aspires.

It is the next level up from influencing someone. The first two levels are about selling your idea to them. This level is about getting them to sell your ideas to the people *they* come in contact with. Imagine how much greater your reach is if everyone you speak to then goes on to spread your message. We want our audience to not just listen to us, not just think about what we say, but to *act*.

Your talk inspires their walk.

It's wonderful to entertain a crowd, or teach them an interesting fact, or lift their spirits for an afternoon. It's exciting to provoke their thoughts, leave them thinking and wondering. But truly, unless they actually do something differently as a result of hearing you speak, the value of what you say is limited. To inspire someone into action, to mobilise the tribe in pursuit of a better world, this is the essence of speakership. It's the ultimate test of your leadership. Does anyone do anything differently as a result of hearing you speak?

People who are inspired by your message are more likely to take action, more likely to share your ideas, and in doing so impact, influence, and inspire those around them.

A heightened awareness of the broader tribe who aren't in the audience, and mastery of your message and method sets you free to transcend the mechanics of your presentation. Truly inspirational speakers operate in this state of 'flow'.

People with the opportunity to see you in full flight will be inspired into movement, to go back into their everyday environments and take concrete steps toward a better way of being, a smarter way of doing.

You will light a spark of inspiration that will carry your people through tough times, motivate them to invest their discretionary energy, and fire them up at the start of each new challenge. That's the purpose of speakership.

MESSAGES THAT MATTER

The art of leadership is the process of influencing people. A key pillar in our quest to master speakership will be our ability to formulate our ideas into powerful memes—ideas that are easy to learn, easy to remember, and easy to spread.

The word 'meme' was first coined by evolutionary biologist Dr Richard Dawkins, for use in his 1976 book *The Selfish Gene*. His purpose was to illustrate that an idea—a meme—spreads through the population in a manner very similar to that in which the genetic characteristics of organisms spread through the population via genes. Through processes of natural selection and popularity the most successful memes stand the test of time.

The Darwinian concept of 'survival of the fittest' provides a neat summary of the process of natural selection. The spread of ideas through the meme pool is very similar, and you can see it in action every day. The chorus of that simple, catchy pop song which you're singing along to. The hilarious joke you're told by a friend which you subsequently tell at the dinner table with family, out at lunch with friends, and at the next work meeting, is another strong meme which spreads quickly through the meme pool.

There are many characteristics that contribute to a powerful meme. A few examples include:

- Easy to learn

- Easy to remember

- Easy to repeat to others

- Appeals to many kinds of people

One element of truth that pops out of the list above is the reality that simple ideas often make the strongest memes. Complex and complicated ideas that require a lot of cognitive focus to digest and understand are naturally weaker memes than simple ideas which can be understood with a minimum of effort.

The common lament that popular music is mostly simple, derivative, and boring is a direct result of this effect. Pop songs have to capture their audience with a single exposure or be forever banished from the radio. Conversely, it can take five, ten, or more listens to a complex sonata before the true beauty of the piece can be understood, a time commitment too great for many people to bother. Consequently, the size of the audience influenced by this meme is severely limited. This is how 'survival of the fittest' applies in the world of art.

The strongest memes last generations, their message distilled into a succinct and pure expression of their intent. It's unlikely you can read the phrase "I have a dream" without immediately conjuring a whole host of associated messages, memories, and feelings. Dr Martin Luther King took a whole movement; a long and complicated history, and through masterful speakership delivered the thrust of the message with a simple, memorable, incredibly powerful statement that would echo through the ages. That's a very potent meme in action.

Two words from Latin—*carpe diem*—carry an important idea understood by millions. Sieze the day. This simple meme has impacted the lives of millions of people, who have used the inspirational meaning wrapped into two words from an ancient language, to make brave positive choices when faced with a dilemma. It's a whole life philosophy distilled into a tiny phrase.

This demand for simplicity is key to grabbing attention, getting heard and making a difference. Oliver Wendell Holmes once remarked, "'I could not give a fig for simplicity this side of complexity but I would give my left arm for simplicity on the other side of complexity."

The challenge for leaders and aspiring leaders is that some messages are not simple and we don't want to dumb them down. Messages that matter can't always be packaged neatly into a three word slogan. Einstein famously said, 'things should be as simple as possible, and no simpler'.

It's this simplicity spectrum that you must address. How can you retain the integrity of an idea in the process of simplification? How can you 'smarten the idea down'? Great leaders dance between the abstract and the concrete when they speak; making points that are simple yet elegant, concise yet complete.

Those who excel at Speakership ruthlessly prune their speeches and presentations to make sure they are packed with messages that matter.

Navigation

The majority of the rest of this book is going to dive deeply into the creation, formation and refinement of your *message* and explore the many ways you can bring it to life through your *method* of delivery.

There are nine practical principles of speakership that apply in every speaking situation. If you're a leader addressing your own teams, an employee speaking to the wider company about an idea you've had, or a CEO speaking to an industry conference, the principles apply. It doesn't matter if your talk is 15 minutes or 50 minutes. The nine practical principles guide you through message, method and mastery enabling you to nail speakership as your newest leadership capability.

Message

Message is the foundation of speakership. Like temple bells that continue to ring out long after they have first been rung, whenever you speak you want your message to have a lasting impact, resonating in the minds of the audience long after your presentation is over. Crafting memorable ideas, sharing from your expertise and unique personal experiences, is at the heart of creating a compelling speech. A truly powerful message can be understood quickly and shared easily. Building a message that matters is the first step in every rock star presentation.

In this section we're going to recommend you spend hour upon countless hour rigorously formulating, testing, repacking, and refining your ideas; and we'll give you the frameworks you need to successfully achieve that.

The three principles in Message are *Command the context*, *Unpack your genius*, and *Build time capsules*.

Method

Delivering your message in way that ignites and inspires your audience is the fast track to maximum impact and influence. It's about taking your ideas and breathing life into them through edutainment. Mixing up the learning with laughter. Punctuating your points with punch lines. Bringing contrast and colour through dramatic use of voice, facial expressions and carefully choreographed movement. It's paradoxically about turning up in your most authentic, charismatic state to transform the theoretical or academic into something dynamic and powerful. Meaningful and memorable. It's achieved by making your presentation a performance.

This section of the book provides a practical framework that will help you make them laugh, make them think, and make them care.

The three principles in Method are *Amplify your self*, *Entertain the crowd*, and *Work the room*.

Mastery

Mastery describes the ability of a world class presenter to control their focus and awareness in service of the room. It is the intuition that is born from experience. When you message is clear and elegantly crafted and your delivery inspirational and entertaining, it's mastery that enables you to gauge the collective emotional state of the room and make subtle adjustments to better meet the needs of your audience. Speakers in mastery are in flow, synchronised with the audience, set free from ego and fully present to the co-created experience they are leading. Mastery doesn't come from striving, it is enabled when you surrender.

The three principles in Mastery are *Choose your state*, *Expand your awareness*, and *Get out of the way*.

PRINCIPLE 1

Command
the context

The first thing to do before you begin any work on your presentation is to make sure you are clear what your speech is about, at a high level. The risk is that you talk about too much, over prepare, and lose people by trying to cover too many topics with your message.

Like many things in life, your presentation will need focus to achieve cut-through. This maxim is more relevant than ever now that the audience has a world of distractions in the palm of their hand. Today's audience is a living node in a network of others. Your audience is now beyond the ballroom and in the corridors of social media, often while you speak.

You need to answer the critical question "What is it you are talking about?" In fact, this question is often better delivered from its opposite perspective; "What does your audience need to hear?" If you're not clear about your message, how can your audience ever hope to be?

As a leader, it's your job to create clarity from confusion, turn fear into confidence, and mobilise people in pursuit of a better future. When you set out to develop memorable messages you have to make decisions about what's truly worth talking about and what the audience in the room and the wider tribe need to hear. More specifically, what do they need to hear from *you*? How can you best serve them in way no-one else in the organisation could?

As leaders and chiefs we are tasked with making sense of what's going on around us and creating contextual clarity so our people have a clear path forward. The advertised topic might be 'developing a high performance team' but the context for your message could be 'meritocracy'. The situation you're speaking in might be around 'cost cutting measures' but the context for your presentation is 'growth' or 'opportunity'.

Context is the 'big word'. Commanding context is the first big idea in the speakership curriculum. If you can boil the essence of your presentation down into one word, you are starting to command the context. If you command the context you control the conversation, and more importantly for leaders you start to frame the dialogue in ways that provide solutions and direction.

You command context for three main reasons:

1. It's efficient. You won't waste time messing around preparing content that has no place being in your speech.

2. It's effective. People have little room in their mind to pay attention. Keep everything relevant to your central theme, and you have a better chance of being heard.

3. It's leveraged. Audiences probably won't remember what you said, but if you nail the context they will remember what it was about. This means they can share your big idea. Not only do they get it, but if you really nail context they can share it using their own relevant stories and personal experiences.

It's a matter of working out what you're truly talking about. Not the details of the content, but the higher meaning of the message as you rise through layers of abstraction. This is not the time to be specific. In the big-picture planning phase, don't rush into case studies, facts or stories. Right now your job is to scope out the big ideas for the presentation so that everything you say fits congruently into that theme. You need to build from the top down, not the bottom up.

SPEECH ON AN ENVELOPE

A great practice to develop is the skill of sketching the framework of your speech on the back of an envelope. The limited space on an envelope forces you to work at the contextual level. The finished product will look a bit like this:

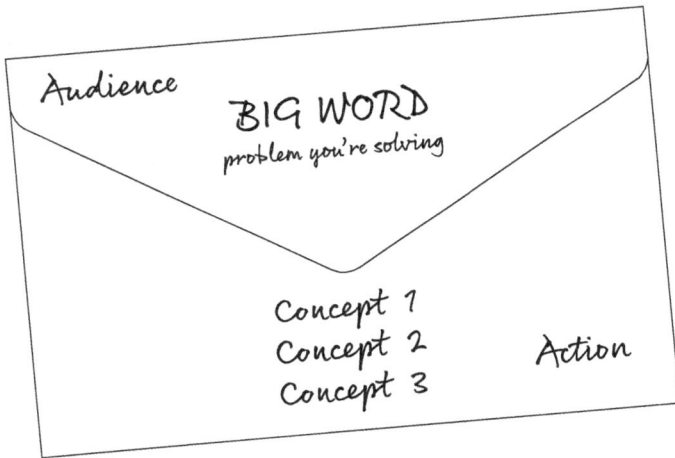

Now, while you are reading this book, quickly grab an envelope. It can actually be a piece of fresh paper, your moleskin notebook, or a document in your computer, but the back of an envelope has a certain romantic appeal.

At the top, write down the word which captures the essence of your presentation. It's typically a high-level one word theme. Your word is not the theme of the gathering, it's the theme of your speech. Perhaps you're at a conference about 'service', and your speech is about 'loyalty'. Or a 'planning' meeting which you think is really about 'execution'. Remember not to live down in the concrete. "Increase sales by 10%" is not a theme. Once you've identified the word, write that down at the top of the envelope.

No speech should ever be delivered without a clear picture of the target audience in mind. If you're going to act in their service, you need to know who they are. Use the top left of the envelope to capture who they are and maybe a few defining qualities about how they think, work or play.

Now comes the crux of the speech. Now you need to focus on what problem you're solving. The problem goes right under the big idea. The problem needs to be relevant to the target audience *and* aligned to the contextual theme. *Everything* we do on this envelope needs to live congruently under the big word at the top.

It can also help to think about the problem in both a towards- and away-from orientation. This will enable you to articulate it as both an aspiration 'here is what we would like' and a problem 'here is what we want to fix'. Don't worry if it sounds repetitive.

Now it's time to think about what question your speech is answering. This may feel a little redundant as you are revisiting the problem and aspiration from the previous step, although sometimes the audience isn't fully aware of the problem they're faced with so the question they're asking might be a bit different. Don't worry if the questions and problems you're writing seem similar, they're not redundant. Overlapping is good, it's a tightening and refining of the speech. By viewing your speech from each of these different perspectives, you'll better understand how to align your content to the overarching contextual theme.

We've now completed four major steps on the envelope; big word, problem, target audience and question. Next we scribble down the key ideas that will make up your speech. You should end up with 3, 5, or maybe 7 points that nest under your big word and address the question and problem. Stay on point.

Finally, you need to plan your speech so that it sits congruently with two more contextual themes;

1. The agenda of the conference or focus of the meeting; otherwise you run the risk of being deemed irrelevant, and;

2. Your personal big word (the next section of the book details this idea).

The ultimate speech for the situation is *your* word (as the speaker), delivered through *their* word.

When asked about the incredible beauty of the statue of David, Michelangelo is said to have remarked that he simply removed everything that wasn't David. Starting with that enormous block of marble, he chipped away until what was left was the essence of David and nothing more. He never took away too much, and he never slapped clay back on. It was as minimal as it could be. Every piece of material left is a crucial piece of David.

Those words on your envelope, simple but profound, are the statue of David of your speech. In order to craft a beautiful, elegant, and inspiring speech you say nothing that doesn't contribute to and elevate those words. By delivering a speech guided by the contextual themes that matter, you will create something far more relevant and moving than you would by just assembling some relevant stuff. There's an appropriate quotation variously attributed to Churchill, Twain, and Woodrow Wilson, among others: "If you want me to give a five hour speech, give me five minutes to prepare. If you want me to give a five minute speech, give me five hours to prepare".

Delivering just the marble, with no clay slapped on the outside, nothing unnecessary or inconsequential, is crucial to powerful presentations. The envelope is the tool you use to work out what's marble, and what's just clay. The envelope gives you incredible clarity around your message and what you're trying to convey to the audience.

Of course, most organisations and meeting planners won't do you the courtesy of summarising the context of their agenda in a single word, so you'll likely need to work it out based on your dealings with them. If you believe their word is *service* and yours is *wellbeing*, you could deliver a great speech about providing excellent service by looking after people's needs. If their word is *engagement* and yours is *excite*, you could craft an incredible message around how to provide an engaging way of sharing the customer's excitement with them. If your word, on the other hand, is *presence*, you could talk about how the business must really listen to the customer's needs, and that engagement is really about being present to the customers' opinions and feelings.

As you start to think about your key messages and the higher context you also need to consider the unique contribution that you bring to that message. Who are you when you're at the front of the room and how does that align with your key messages?

Principle 1 Command the context

WHAT'S *YOUR* BIG WORD?

It's worth taking some time to understand *your* context, not just the context of the speech. We're going to go even deeper.

One of the most important elements of a compelling speech is conviction. If the speaker is not completely convinced by their message, the audience will tune out immediately. People have an incredible capacity for sensing integrity and they'll never believe a word that comes out of the mouth of someone they find wanting in that department.

Whenever you speak, whatever the topic, you must come from a place of integrity. You must speak with the conviction of someone in total alignment with the message they are spreading. It doesn't matter if you're speaking about motivation, or optimism, or sales data, or marketing strategy, or anything else. Perhaps you speak on a number of different topics. You can speak with authority about anything so long as your message is congruent with your inner purpose, aligned with your authentic self.

Fear not, cynics, this book is not about to jump the shark and wander off on a bizarre spiritual tangent. As you'll discover as you work your way through this book, we place an enormous premium on the contextual themes that accompany ideas, as we know that people are subconsciously guided and influenced by the themes they consider important in their own lives.

Without a well-considered contextual theme, it's very difficult to compose a message with compelling purpose. We believe most leaders spend way too much time concentrating on 'stuff' and nowhere near enough time wondering what it's all really about. They give speeches that could have been written by anyone. Stepping into speakership means bringing the very best of you, the real you, to your messages. Your audiences, your teams, your wider tribe long to get a sense of who you are. Remember they are deciding whether or not to follow you. Your message and who you are must align. This major step on the ultimate personal development journey asks a very important question:

What are *you* all about?

What's your higher purpose? Sure, your current work might be focused on the benefits of implementing risk mitigation procedures in corporate expansion strategy, but that's probably not what you'd be thinking about if you were told you only had three months left to live. You might spend a bunch of your time describing the health benefits of legumes to people, but you probably don't dream about that while staring at the sea from a windswept clifftop.

If you had to describe your purpose in life, what would it be? If you had to identify the single common thread that has connected everything you've ever done, what would it be? If you had to distil your life down to a single word, what would it be?

This word then becomes the culmination of your life's experience. It's the lens through which everything you've ever done makes sense. It's the congruent filter through which your expertise across any number of subjects is powerfully aligned. Be warned, though; your life theme cannot be located in your resumé. You might have spent a lot of time as a health professional, but your word isn't "doctor". You might have spent plenty of time in court, but your word isn't "law".

Your word is higher, more abstract than that. Your word isn't the content of your life, it is the context of your life.

Asimov's word might have been *possibility*. Jobs: *perfection*. Branson: *adventure*. One particularly famous and influential modern orator actually published his word on a poster with his face, as part of an election campaign: *hope*.

Obama is in fact a perfect case study for this exercise, and the acceptance speech he delivered when he won the US Presidential election in 2008 demonstrates how contextual words frame the content of what we actually say. Here we've reproduced the speech in its entirety, and above each paragraph placed the contextual word that sits above the content of that section. It's an exercise that will hopefully help you start to see the themes that we all sense when we hear a speech being given, even if we don't consciously notice and name them.

Barack Obama
Presidential Acceptance Speech

──────── SIGNIFICANCE ────────

If there is anyone out there who still doubts that America is a place where all things are possible; who still wonders if the dream of our founders is alive in our time; who still questions the power of our democracy, tonight is your answer.

It's the answer told by lines that stretched around schools and churches in numbers this nation has never seen; by people who waited three hours and four hours, many for the very first time in their lives, because they believed that this time must be different; that their voice could be that difference.

──────── DIVERSITY ────────

It's the answer spoken by young and old, rich and poor, Democrat and Republican, black, white, Latino, Asian, Native American, gay, straight, disabled and not disabled—Americans who sent a message to the world that we have never been a collection of Red States and Blue States: we are, and always will be, the United States of America.

——————— HOPE ———————

It's the answer that led those who have been told for so long by so many to be cynical, and fearful, and doubtful of what we can achieve to put their hands on the arc of history and bend it once more toward the hope of a better day.

——————— SIGNIFICANCE ———————

It's been a long time coming, but tonight, because of what we did on this day, in this election, at this defining moment, change has come to America.

——————— RESPECT ———————

I just received a very gracious call from Senator McCain. He fought long and hard in this campaign, and he's fought even longer and harder for the country he loves. He has endured sacrifices for America that most of us cannot begin to imagine, and we are better off for the service rendered by this brave and selfless leader. I congratulate him and Governor Palin for all they have achieved, and I look forward to working with them to renew this nation's promise in the months ahead.

——————— GRATITUDE ———————

I want to thank my partner in this journey, a man who campaigned from his heart and spoke for the men and women he grew up with on the streets of Scranton and rode with on that train home to Delaware, the Vice President-elect of the United States, Joe Biden.

I would not be standing here tonight without the unyielding support of my best friend for the last sixteen years, the rock of our family and the love of my life, our nation's next First Lady, Michelle Obama. Sasha and Malia, I love you both so much, and you have earned the new puppy that's coming with us to the White House. And while she's no longer with us, I know my grandmother is watching, along with the family that made me who I am. I miss them tonight, and know that my debt to them is beyond measure.

To my campaign manager David Plouffe, my chief strategist David Axelrod, and the best campaign team ever assembled in the history of politics—you made this happen, and I am forever grateful for what you've sacrificed to get it done.

HUMILITY

But above all, I will never forget who this victory truly belongs to—it belongs to you.

I was never the likeliest candidate for this office. We didn't start with much money or many endorsements. Our campaign was not hatched in the halls of Washington—it began in the backyards of Des Moines and the living rooms of Concord and the front porches of Charleston.

SERVICE

It was built by working men and women who dug into what little savings they had to give five dollars and ten dollars and twenty dollars to this cause. It grew strength from the young people who rejected the myth of their generation's apathy; who left their homes and their families for jobs that offered little pay and less sleep; from the not-so- young people who braved the bitter cold and scorching heat to knock on the doors of perfect strangers; from the millions of Americans who volunteered, and organized, and proved that more than two centuries later, a government of the people, by the people and for the people has not perished from this Earth. This is your victory.

I know you didn't do this just to win an election and I know you didn't do it for me. You did it because you understand the enormity of the task that lies ahead. For even as we celebrate tonight, we know the challenges that tomorrow will bring are the greatest of our lifetime—two wars, a planet in peril, the worst financial crisis in a century. Even as we stand here tonight, we know there are brave Americans waking up in the deserts of Iraq and the mountains of Afghanistan to risk their lives for us. There are mothers and fathers who will lie awake after their children fall asleep and wonder how they'll make the mortgage, or pay their doctor's bills, or save enough for college. There is new energy to harness and new jobs to be created; new schools to build and threats to meet and alliances to repair.

———————— EXPECTATION ————————

The road ahead will be long. Our climb will be steep. We may not get there in one year or even one term, but America—I have never been more hopeful than I am tonight that we will get there. I promise you—we as a people will get there.

There will be setbacks and false starts. There are many who won't agree with every decision or policy I make as President, and we know that government can't solve every problem. But I will always be honest with you about the challenges we face. I will listen to you, especially when we disagree. And above all, I will ask you join in the work of remaking this nation the only way it's been done in America for two- hundred and twenty-one years—block by block, brick by brick, calloused hand by calloused hand.

─────── PERSEVERANCE ───────

What began twenty-one months ago in the depths of winter must not end on this autumn night. This victory alone is not the change we seek—it is only the chance for us to make that change. And that cannot happen if we go back to the way things were. It cannot happen without you.

─────── RESPONSIBILITY ───────

So let us summon a new spirit of patriotism; of service and responsibility where each of us resolves to pitch in and work harder and look after not only ourselves, but each other. Let us remember that if this financial crisis taught us anything, it's that we cannot have a thriving Wall Street while Main Street suffers—in this country, we rise or fall as one nation; as one people.

─────── UNITY (LOCAL) ───────

Let us resist the temptation to fall back on the same partisanship and pettiness and immaturity that has poisoned our politics for so long. Let us remember that it was a man from this state who first carried the banner of the Republican Party to the White House—a party founded on the values of self-reliance, individual liberty, and national unity. Those are values we all share, and while the Democratic Party has won a great victory tonight, we do so with a measure of humility and determination to heal the divides that have held back our progress. As Lincoln said to a nation far more divided than ours, "We are not enemies, but friends... though passion may have strained it must not break our bonds of affection." And to those Americans whose support I have yet to earn—I may not have won your vote, but I hear your voices, I need your help, and I will be your President too.

──────── UNITY (GLOBAL) ────────

And to all those watching tonight from beyond our shores, from parliaments and palaces to those who are huddled around radios in the forgotten corners of our world—our stories are singular, but our destiny is shared, and a new dawn of American leadership is at hand. To those who would tear this world down—we will defeat you. To those who seek peace and security—we support you. And to all those who have wondered if America's beacon still burns as bright—tonight we proved once more that the true strength of our nation comes not from our the might of our arms or the scale of our wealth, but from the enduring power of our ideals: democracy, liberty, opportunity, and unyielding hope.

──────── PRIDE ────────

For that is the true genius of America—that America can change. Our union can be perfected. And what we have already achieved gives us hope for what we can and must achieve tomorrow.

──────── SOLIDARITY ────────

This election had many firsts and many stories that will be told for generations. But one that's on my mind tonight is about a woman who cast her ballot in Atlanta. She's a lot like the millions of others who stood in line to make their voice heard in this election except for one thing—Ann Nixon Cooper is 106 years old.

She was born just a generation past slavery; a time when there were no cars on the road or planes in the sky; when someone like her couldn't vote for two reasons—because she was a woman and because of the color of her skin.

―――――――――― HOPE ――――――――――

And tonight, I think about all that she's seen throughout her century in America—the heartache and the hope; the struggle and the progress; the times we were told that we can't, and the people who pressed on with that American creed: Yes we can.

At a time when women's voices were silenced and their hopes dismissed, she lived to see them stand up and speak out and reach for the ballot. Yes we can.

When there was despair in the dust bowl and depression across the land, she saw a nation conquer fear itself with a New Deal, new jobs and a new sense of common purpose. Yes we can.

When the bombs fell on our harbor and tyranny threatened the world, she was there to witness a generation rise to greatness and a democracy was saved. Yes we can.

She was there for the buses in Montgomery, the hoses in Birmingham, a bridge in Selma, and a preacher from Atlanta who told a people that "We Shall Overcome." Yes we can.

A man touched down on the moon, a wall came down in Berlin, a world was connected by our own science and imagination. And this year, in this election, she touched her finger to a screen, and cast her vote, because after 106 years in America, through the best of times and the darkest of hours, she knows how America can change. Yes we can.

America, we have come so far. We have seen so much. But there is so much more to do. So tonight, let us ask ourselves—if our children should live to see the next century;

if my daughters should be so lucky to live as long as Ann Nixon Cooper, what change will they see? What progress will we have made?

———————— INSPIRATION ————————

This is our chance to answer that call. This is our moment. This is our time—to put our people back to work and open doors of opportunity for our kids; to restore prosperity and promote the cause of peace; to reclaim the American Dream and reaffirm that fundamental truth—that out of many, we are one; that while we breathe, we hope, and where we are met with cynicism, and doubt, and those who tell us that we can't, we will respond with that timeless creed that sums up the spirit of a people: Yes we can.

———————— TRADITION ————————

Thank you, God bless you, and may God Bless the United States of America.

Here we can see Obama's speech summarised in a few important, powerful themes. And it's clear the speech as a whole, and especially the themes outlined within it, are completely congruent with Obama's word; *hope*. This congruency is what makes it a powerful speech. If Obama's word was *power*, this would not be a contextually or thematically congruent speech and the response would not have been as positive.

For most people, choosing a word is not a quick or easy process. It requires you to really agonise over the meaning of your life, and interrogate the choices you've made and the things you've done in the past. Choosing a word that congruently describes your purpose over that period is a difficult task. Don't be put off, we believe the payoff is worth the effort.

So what *is* the payoff? Why should you pick a word to describe your higher purpose in life? What's this all about?

Identifying your word and giving it a name means you can speak on *any* topic without being a charlatan. You can speak with conviction. Obama can speak across a broad number of topics with great insight and clarity, because he puts it through the filter of hope. His least convincing moments as a President have been those when what was coming out of his mouth seemed at cross-purposes with his big word. It seemed occasionally the reality of being the President required him to say some things which perhaps he would have preferred not to. Talking about killing insurgents with drones is difficult to frame in the context of 'hope', and thus we in the audience sense a bit of incongruence about him in these moments.

Your big word becomes a powerful lens through which you can speak on a great many topics, and serves as a highly effective early warning system. If ever you are asked to speak on a topic that you cannot filter through your big word, you know not to speak on that topic. It's too far removed from your purpose as a person that you will not deliver the message, whatever it might be, with total conviction.

Remember, however, that your word is not designed to limit you. It's actually a tool to give you *greater* flexibility when you speak, because you can speak through your word, rather than refuse a request for a particular topic. For example, if your word is engagement and you're asked "Can you speak about customer service?" your response is "Yes, I can talk about engagement and how that affects customer service". Your word is the lens through which everything you speak about is focused and filtered, and it provides a powerful and effective method of speaking from a place of total conviction across an incredibly broad range of topics.

As a leader, once you've identified your big word you can combine what your people need to hear from you with the unique angle you bring to deliver memorable messages. You can help them make sense of a situation by bringing contextual clarity that is aligned with who you are, and your core life's purpose.

Matt's big word is *leverage*, Col's is *play*, and Sacha's is *fearless*. Every talk, speech, presentation we ever give, to our own people and to much larger groups outside of our own organisations, gets filtered through those individual words.

PRINCIPLE 2

Unpack your genius

What do you know?

We reckon heaps more than you let yourself believe. It's likely you have forgotten more great ideas than a person can implement in their lifetime. This is both inspiring (in the sense that the human mind has incredible potential) and sad (in the sense that most great thinking gets lost and goes to waste).

Why do we do this? Why is it that most great leaders have forgotten more great ideas than ones they can remember? It comes down to modern memes; "just in time" and "fit for purpose". Two great ideas that are entirely unhelpful in this circumstance.

We tend to commit the effort to thinking only when we have a problem to solve (ie; just in time), and while this sounds like an efficient use of time it's actually like living hand to mouth.

We also tend to create our ideas for a specific delivery (ie; fit for purpose). We write books and speeches, emails and meeting notes, but we don't store *ideas*. In business we've gotten very comfortable with the idea of "build once and sell often", in the Thought Leaders community we teach you to *think* once and *use* often.

Let's stop wasting genius. Let's capture it and store it in an ideas bank, so you or others can access it and share it when the time is right.

So what do you know about? What's in your head? What do you know that can help your people? What can you share that will challenge and motivate them? What can you teach them?

IDEA BANK

Leadership. Collaboration. Engagement. Innovation. Growth mindsets. Sales strategy. Global marketing. Empowerment. Financial Literacy. Management for Millennials. Survival strategies for the digital age. Project management. Accounting for the clueless. Future trends. Essentials of emotional intelligence.

Thought leaders develop a bank of thoughts or ideas that can be accessed in a moment and can be instantly customised to suit any audience or situation. They become a living encyclopaedia of knowledge and expertise, filled with experience and insight in service of the people around them. To achieve this, you need to capture the essence of an idea quickly and have a system to deposit, review, and withdraw them as required.

We believe that you should never speak about something unless you have given it considerable thought. Even when faced with a spontaneous request to speak, you can still speak from a well-considered space, assuming you have done some prep work on your *Idea Bank*.

An *Idea Bank* is constantly being enhanced, re-worked and customised. It is a well organised, chunked down catalogue of mini presentations. The IP snapshot system we teach in the Thought Leaders Business School allows for different people to deliver the same message and adjust it for their style and environment.

Seven benefits of an Idea Bank are:

1. You can speedily prepare a great presentation

2. You are free to customise content whilst preparing

3. You can extend or shorten the duration
   of your speech as required

4. You don't have to rehearse speeches to be word perfect

5. You demonstrate your knowledge
   impressively when asked to speak

6. Other people can present the same message and
   adjust the content to suit their personal style, and

7. Idea fragments can be saved for future inquiry.

In short, it's about creating a set of key ideas and messages that you draw upon at different times and present in a different sequence depending on the outcome you are looking to achieve.

The ideas in your bank are all valued differently; some are big ideas, some smaller. A presentation may need a few smaller ideas to make the big ones work. The more ideas you have in your bank the better, but only if you can access them easily. Here's the seven steps to creating an idea bank and the first look at the how-to tools.

Seven steps to creating an idea bank

Step 1: Create a list
Write a numbered list of all the things you know, talk on, or may like to talk on. If they are across several fields of expertise, then build a list for each field of expertise.

Step 2: Identify Idea Clusters
Know the difference between an idea and a cluster of ideas. An idea has only a few key points associated with it. If you brainstormed all the points around your idea and came up with more than three points, it's probably a few ideas clustered together. Break the cluster down or chunk it up until you have a clear idea that has, for example, three central points.

Step 3: Have a point

Be clear on the point of your idea. We call this the concept. You should be able to summarise your idea as one or two simple sentences that explain the whole point. From this singular idea, you then create several different ways of saying it.

Tools for Concept:

1. Declarative and explanatory sentences.

2. Mantras and slogans.

3. Palette variety.

Step 4: Make it a big idea

Try to identify the essence of the idea. How does it fit into the big picture? Often this is a diagram, model, metaphor, an allegory or some applicable quotes. Ideally, you will have a 'big word' associated with this idea, for use in the 'back of the envelope' exercise.

Tools for Context:

1. Model or diagram

2. Metaphor or analogy

3. Quotes and allegories

Step 5: Support your point

Gather examples, facts, stories and other detail elements to support or explain your point. We call this content. Like the big idea, you need to balance this to cover the whole brain.

Tools for Content:

1. Stories

2. Case Studies and examples

3. Statistics and step-by-step processes

Step 6: Create a system

Document the idea in a searchable, retrievable system. This can be as simple as a filing cabinet or more preferably in a digital world, an application that allows quick and easy retrieval using search terms and tags. Evernote is a good example.

Step 7: Customise content, not context

Finally, constantly review your *Idea Bank*—particularly in the content area. It is the content that changes most, not the concept or the context. If you clearly think out concepts and can represent them in any context, then all you need to worry about is what content you will use to create a connection with your audience. Getting good at this allows you to repeat key ideas over and over, with people hearing them again as if for the first time. This is the essence of **Principle 3**: *Build time capsules.*

Your Idea Bank is your go-to source for inspiration and forms the basis of every speech you'll ever make. It's a repository of all your ideas, your key messages, the points you want to make, fleshed out across the roles of a speaker and across the full thinking spectrum: analytical/creative and abstract/concrete.

FULL SPECTRUM THINKING

Any time you communicate, your message sits somewhere on a spectrum between informative and inspirational, and logical and emotional. Some presentations are designed to inspire the audience to take action, to shine new light on a subject and instigate change. Other times, the audience is already convinced, and it's more appropriate to provide the information they need to act effectively.

You want to have a keen sense for where on this spectrum your audience resides, and it can shift even as you speak. If an audience is not feeling energised and inspired, you need to bring your speech back up to the inspiration spectrum until you've got them excited and re-energised, before you can dive back down into the information and content.

It's a dance, a balancing act. Your third eye awareness, the ability to sense the engagement of the audience even as you're working through your presentation, is the key here. If ever you sense you've lost the audience, they're looking distracted or disengaged, you'll want to reintroduce some energy and inspiration to your speech until you've got them back in your pocket. A great presentation delivered with mastery is not a rigid form. It's a fluid, dynamic creation that will be different every time you deliver it, based on the response of each particular audience.

As you prepare your message you'll be thinking about how to nimbly move between information and inspiration.

Overlaid with the spectrum from inspire to inform, your audience will also lay on a spectrum between "heads and hearts", the logical and emotional. Often this is referred to as left and right brain thinking. Left brain is analytical, scientific, and cynical; right brain is more emotional, creative, and optimistic. All your content will lay somewhere on this spectrum.

The results summary of a data-heavy case study, for example, is very left brain. The story about the time you hiked the Andes—which serves as a metaphor for hard work—is very right brain.

Your audience may tend one way or the other because of their demographic and psychographic profile (consider the difference between a chartered accountants conference and a graphic design summit), or because the presentations and activities that have gone before you leave them primed for a certain message. Like the inspire-inform spectrum, you want to make sure that your messages are articulated in a way that touches both heads and hearts.

You'll win the battle for hearts and minds when you design memorable messages that speak to each quadrant on the spectrum. Think about the talks you've most recently given. Has your message ranged from information to inspiration, and from hearts to minds? Have you moved fluidly between all four as you respond to the needs of your audience?

Inspire

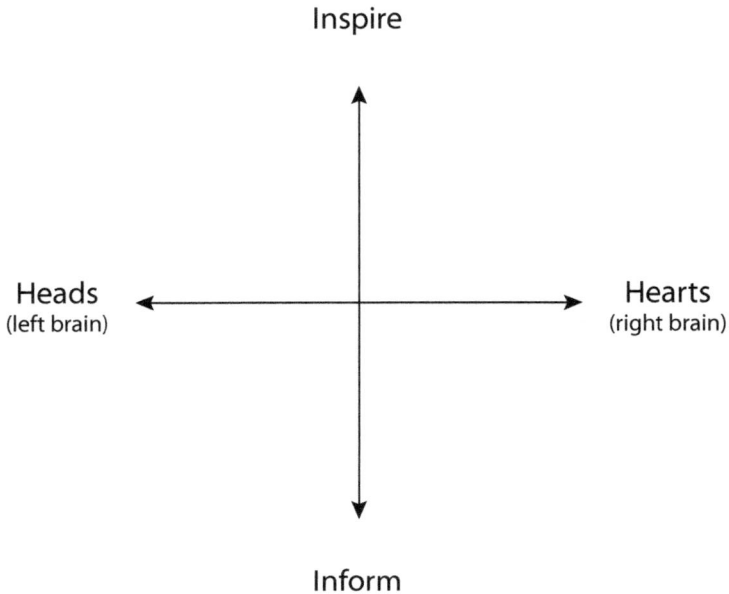

Heads
(left brain)

Hearts
(right brain)

Inform

This simple concept helps us understand how different people think, and to ensure that we formulate and explain our ideas in a way that gives all kinds of people the opportunity to fully comprehend them.

Our ambition in sharing the idea of full-spectrum thinking with you is to expand your understanding of how other people work. This book is in large part a book about leadership, and a leader must spend a lot more time thinking about other people than she does about herself. Personality profiling might be fraught with risk when applied blindly, but if borrowing from the field helps us become better speakers and better leaders, let's take the best bits.

So, now onto capturing your genius.

IP SNAPSHOTS (PINK SHEETS)

IP snapshots are the method by which you can capture and refine your message, building a relevant and elegant bank of ideas that you can draw on at any time. In the Thought Leaders community, we call these IP snapshots 'Pink Sheets'. This methodology was originally created on a pink sheet of paper and the name stuck. Lawyers like yellow pads, Thought Leaders love pink sheets (even though most of them aren't literally pink).

Using the Pink Sheet framework to capture your ideas creates depth in your thinking and forces you to create messages with substance and balance. Each concept or point you want to share will have its own Pink Sheet.

BIG WORD

CONTEXT

Model

Metaphor

CONCEPT

Statement

Explanation

CONTENT

Study

Story

PINK SHEET

thought leaders

Concept

Start in the middle of the page.

Your concept lives in the middle of the Pink Sheet and summarises the point of the idea. The goal of this section of the Pink Sheet is to make you carefully select your words. We've talked about the need to make statements in a way which is memorable, to craft great ideas into powerful memes that spread. The concept layer of the pink sheet is where this process happens. There are three primary ideation strategies we recommend to make this work. You can do one, two, or all three of them. Each will stretch your mind in different directions, with the goal being to uncover something special you didn't realise you had in you.

A/B Statement

This is the most common method of writing your point and it's basically an exercise in imagining what you would name a book if it were about only this one idea. The 'A' statement is the title of the book. Ten words at most, probably less, as you want it to be snappy and memorable. Something that would stand out on a bookshelf. Something that would entice a prospective reader to take a closer look.

The 'B' statement is the byline, the explanatory statement that spells out in a little more detail what the reader would expect to find behind the front cover. The B statement too should be carefully worded. It's the sentence that either will or won't sell the book—the idea—to someone passing by. It needs to have some impact.

To illustrate the point, here are three A/B statements taken from the Pink Sheets used to create this book:

A: Speakership is leadership.

B: Every time you speak in public, you are auditioning for a leadership position.

A: Fix nervous with service.

B: The cure for nervous tension is acting in service of the tribe.

A: Stop wasting genius.

B: Capture and store your genius in an ideas bank, so you can access it and share it when the time is right.

Left brain / right brain

This method also creates two statements, but this time it's about the linguistic palette you use. The two statements should describe the same point, but one with a left brain flavour, and one with a right brain slant. For example:

Left brain: Speakership is the new leadership imperative.

Right brain: Speakership is leading out loud.

These are two statements used regularly throughout this book. Another example is the value statement of Thought Leaders Business School:

Left brain: Earn $500K–$1.5M, working 50–200 days, with 1 or 2 support staff.

Right brain: Do work you love, with people you like, the way you want.

The goal here is to maximise the gap between the two statements. Try to maximise positive tension between the two, even while they're making basically the same point.

7/17/37/70

This is an exercise of using language to make the point appealing to people of widely varying ages. Forcing yourself to stretch the palette of words you use in order to unlock the best possible IP from your mind. The process for this one is straightforward:

> 7: Make it simple. Short, sharp and effective. A 7
> year old needs to understand your message.

> 17: Make it inspiring. Word it so a 17 year old
> would want to take it and show it to the world.

> 37: Make it pragmatic. A parent with two kids under five just
> wants to know what needs to be done and get on with it.

> 70: Make it wise. Say it like an experienced
> old-hand who's been around a while.

Again, here are some examples taken from the Pink Sheets that crafted this book:

> 7: Speakership is leading out loud.

> 17: Speakership is leadership, and every tribe needs a leader.

> 37: Stop managing and start leading; stop
> informing and start inspiring.

> 70: Speakership is the missing link between strategy
> and execution. Between wanting people to do
> something, and inspiring them to take action.

Each of these three strategies can help you unlock the ideas in your head and create memorable phrasing for your ideas that will make them more exciting, easier to remember, and easier to repeat. It's the primary building block of a powerful meme.

Context

At the top of the pink sheet is context, the overarching theme within which this idea lives. Context is characterised by three parts:

1. The model. The model is a diagram which describes where this idea lives in the greater hierarchy. The model might be a Venn diagram, or a ladder, or a circle. It's a tool which helps visually describe the hierarchy of ideas in play and provides a map for navigating them. A single model will often be the 'parent' of (and therefore shared across) a number of pink sheets. A five-rung ladder model would lead to at least five pink sheets.

2. The metaphor. Metaphors are an incredibly powerful way to help people relate to an idea and immediately understand its relationship to the wider issue in play. Metaphors allow the brain to use existing neural pathways and cognitive understanding and immediately apply it in the new context. As a tool for gaining rapid understanding of the significance and importance of an idea, the metaphor is invaluable. Some metaphors will be shared across multiple pink sheets. Some will apply only to one. In his book 'I've Never Metaphor I Didn't Like', Mardy Groth unpacks the history of the most enduring metaphors and offers hundreds of examples from famous thinkers and writers that might stimulate your own ideas.

3. The big word. This is the overarching theme of the idea. If you could use only a single word to describe the significance of the idea, that is the word you would place

here. It's the word that will help you group the appropriate pink sheets together when you're crafting your speech.

Content

The bottom layer of the pink sheet contains the 'stuff'. Here's where the supporting data, case studies, stories, anecdotes and pictures live. Remember that each point should be represented as much as possible by left brain analytical content like data and case studies, along with right brain creative content like stories and anecdotes. Ensuring you have a variety of content across the spectrum means you'll be well equipped to back up each point with compelling and relevant content, cherry picked to suit the audience.

One of the key takeaways for you to consider when learning this IP snapshot process is understanding the layers of thought. There are small ideas—detail and content—which rise through layers of abstraction to the higher levels of understanding. For example:

Small: Hamburger

Medium: Food

Big: Energy

The hamburger is the concrete detail of the idea, but the higher context to consider when hamburgers are in the conversation is energy. Learning to identify the higher contextual ideas that frame your content, and successfully communicate it with your audience, is going to massively increase the strength of your presentations. It helps dispel disagreements of the "he said, she said" kind that tend to be mired in detail and achieve little or nothing. It helps link each of your points into a bigger, more convincing overall argument that more people can understand and identify with. It helps group your points into congruent 'families' that share common themes and build off each other.

So, for each of your ideas you'll need to work out where on the pink sheet the idea lives. Is what you've got the equivalent of 'hamburger', 'food', or 'energy'? Is it content, concept, or context? 'Red bus', 'transport' or 'movement'? Do you need to think up or down (or both) from this starting point? Have you recorded a basic story (right brain, content)? Have you drawn a model (left brain, context)? Thought of a metaphor (right brain, context)? Once you've worked out where on the pink sheet the idea lives, you'll know what thinking needs to be done to flesh it out. You may find that some of your ideas actually belong together on one pink sheet. Perhaps a workplace story beautifully illustrates a concept statement from elsewhere. Perhaps you realise a number of separate points can be tied together into a single overarching model.

It's good to be 'light' in this process. Don't be too concerned with detail and locking things down. Aspire to be playful and try lots of different ways of arranging and connecting information. You may be surprised what wisdom hides within your mind, waiting to be unlocked by the process of stretching yourself out of your usual mode of thinking.

ORGANISING GENIUS

Just like a magnificent building that has both form and function, every presentation needs architectural integrity. It's not enough to have a beginning, middle and end; or just make 5 good points. The structure of your speech, the way you link ideas, and the order you present them makes a massive difference to the outcome. If want to have impact, to influence, and inspire you'll need to carefully design the order of what you say to provide your audience and the wider tribe with a complete, compelling and convincing argument that inspires action.

The Filing Cabinet

Imagine you had all of your pink sheets laid out on a table in front of you. You're going to need a pretty big table. Each idea, each sheet, would have the point written on it—the concept. It would have supporting evidence in the form of data, case studies, anecdotes, stories, and pictures. It would have a model that frames the idea in the context of the whole problem, and a metaphor to help people understand how it relates to the other ideas around it. Importantly, it would have a 'big word' at the top which provides the overarching contextual theme of the idea. That big words aligns with your personal big purpose word. Just look at that table.

You've got a lot of paper. You're going to need a filing cabinet.

Of course, you wouldn't simply stuff everything into the filing cabinet, you would categorise and organise the sheets as you create them, flesh them out, and file them away for future reference.

Everything you know about your topic is going into a standard four-drawer filing cabinet. What are you going to name the drawers?

We suggest that you would label them with the following:

- The Inspiration: Turn me on.

- The Strategy: Show me a map.

- The Tactics: Give me directions.

- The Impact: Show me the future.

The progression from *inspiration* to *strategy*, through *tactics* to *impact* is a logical method by which people can triage information, and is the key path through which a leader can create clarity from confusion, turn fear into confidence, and inspire people to act in pursuit of a common goal.

It makes sense, then, to organise our thoughts, and our speeches in the same manner.

The Inspiration Drawer

The *inspiration* drawer of your cabinet contains all of the IP which is influential. Everything which helps the audience understand why your message is important; everything which is designed to convince them to listen. Everything which spells out the value they would receive by following your advice, is stored in this drawer.

The *inspiration* drawer gives you the commercial angle. It doesn't matter what problem your solution solves, if you can't convince people of the value they will receive by taking action, it will never get put into practice. A really well fleshed-out, comprehensive *inspiration* drawer adds directly to price people would be willing to pay to listen to your advice and follow it. If you're speaking in a commercial environment, a great *inspiration* drawer translates directly into dollars, which is a great motivation to ensure you've done really rigorous thinking in creating your snapshots for this drawer.

Using the full spectrum of thinking is really important when you are in the *inspiration* portion of your presentation. From big pictures to concrete examples, from left brain analytical across to right brain creative, the value of your message must be constructed and delivered right across this spectra.

As leaders speaking to your own audiences, the *inspiration* drawer is absolutely critical. People have limited reserves of motivation. They need to be thoroughly convinced before they will be inspired to action. Whether a teacher inviting children to learn, a doctor convincing parents to vaccinate, or a politician imploring people to vote; you need to clearly describe the benefit the audience will receive by taking action. The *inspiration* drawer is filled with everything designed to influence the audience.

As members of an audience we want to know why we should take this journey. Why should we put in the effort? Why should we change? Why this? Why now? Why you? If your audience doesn't grasp the gravity of the situation, or understand the reward that comes from taking the journey you're inviting them on, you've lost before you've begun. A mind unconvinced is a mind closed. Until you audience is begging to know more you can't move on. Always start your speeches with *inspiration*.

The Strategy Drawer

The *strategy* drawer contains all the snapshots that are enlightening. Once your audience is fully *inspired* around why they should listen and take action, you must give them an overall sense of *strategy* for how they will overcome the problems they face.

The *strategy* drawer contains a map of the full breadth of the problem and solution, and a description of the actions that will be required to get to the ideal solution. This is the overview or map, but not the specific territory or route options. For that we need to move into the next drawer.

The information in the strategy drawer should leave the audience with a clear understanding of what needs to be achieved in order to solve their problems or reach their goals. Whilst they won't yet know each of the specific steps required, they'll understand the true nature of the problem and the process that needs to take place to solve it.

A good *strategy* ties the solution back to the *inspiration* nicely. When the two complement each other well, the audience is not only convinced that action is required, but that the course of action to take is the one laid out in front of them.

The Tactics Drawer

The *tactics* drawer is prescriptive. This is where you tell people what to do, detailing the exact steps required to solve the problems they face and get to the solution you promised. Your audience is highly motivated to take action thanks to the compelling reasons you provided in *inspiration*, and understands the scope of the solution mapped out for them in a clear and concise manner in *strategy*.

The *tactics* drawer is often the thickest, with the most snapshots filed within, because it contains lots of fine detail, frameworks, check-lists, and so on; it contains the exact process by which your expertise on the topic will help the audience. Critically, many speakers are most energised by the information in their *tactics* drawer, because this is where they've done most of their work. They know, from experience, that the information in this drawer is where the real value is, this is the stuff that will make an actual physical difference in the lives of their audience.

As a result, most speakers are far too keen to get into the *tactics* drawer when they have the chance to speak. They get too excited by their own content and forget the needs of the audience. So while the *tactics* drawer might contain the message that you're convinced is going to change the world, until you have *inspired* the audience to understand why they should listen to you and shown *strategies* that illustrate how they will put your advice into action, they simply aren't ready for your minutiae, no matter how world-class it may be.

The basic truth is, many speeches, presentations and conversations never get to the point where the *tactics* drawer becomes relevant. In fact, they almost certainly shouldn't. The prescriptive steps required can be delivered in many ways—a booklet to take home, a follow-up training program, a weekly coaching session. A speech or presentation to a room should be spent almost entirely in *inspiration* and *strategy*, so that the audience leaves convinced that action is required, and with an understanding of where to look for the next logical step. They can learn the details of the process later. Your time is best spent ensuring they are truly *inspired* as to why they should put in the effort.

The Impact Drawer

Finally, the *impact* drawer is consequential. The *impact* drawer contains pink sheets which detail the consequences of acting or not acting. It describes the possible future based on the decisions made and actions taken. It details the potential success, and the potential failure. It shows the alternative futures faced by the audience and reinforces the benefit and value they will receive for making the decisions you suggest and taking the actions you prescribe.

You might notice that there's a pretty strong relationship between *inspiration* and *impact*, and between *strategy* and *tactics*, but it's important to separate each of them because while they both seek to achieve the same goal, the nuance of difference between them is important.

It makes sense if you think of it as a journey:

- Inspiration: Tell me why I should take this journey

- Strategy: Show me a map of the journey we might take

- Tactics: Show me the precise route you advise

- Impact: Tell me what I'll find when I get there

It's worth remembering that what's filling the filing cabinet is a lifetime of experience. It's your big word unpacked, your life theme. You're not simply making something up; you're capturing all of your knowledge, wisdom and experience; packaging it up and collating it into a body of work that can be taught, leveraged, and delivered into the world in a million different ways. Imagine your filing cabinet as your PhD research on the topic—but rather than being a 100,000 word document that no-one will ever read, it's a beautifully arranged collection of discrete ideas, concepts, steps, and processes that can be accessed and applied by anyone faced with the problems you know how to solve.

Leadership is inspiring others to action in pursuit of a common goal. The enemy of leadership is 'business as usual'. If you fill each drawer of your filing cabinet with IP snapshots of rigorous, full-spectrum thinking, and then develop architectural integrity in your speeches by structuring them in a carefully arranged order following the *inspiration, strategy, tactics, impact* process, you will almost certainly generate the influence required to smash the status quo and set your audience on a path to change. This is speakership.

GENERATING GENIUS

Now that we know how to capture it and how to store it, let's see if we can get your genius flowing.

Your audience and wider tribe want to hear from your experience, your expertise. They're keen for your reckons and recommendations. Coming up with 10 fully fleshed Pink Sheets might not be so hard, but what about the next 10? The next 25? Getting rockstar good at speaking to groups and leading from the front involves having a large ideas bank to draw from. As a speaker you owe it the audience and the rest of the world to spread the most well-conceived and considered messages that you're capable of creating. How do you go about building your idea bank from day to day?

Imagine yourself as a gemstone collector, searching for the fabled "diamond in the rough". There are rocks of all shapes and sizes in the field through which you're searching, and you know that beneath the surface, some of them are diamonds. Of course, you wouldn't try to cut and polish each and every rock and try to turn it into jewellery right there in the field. You'd take a satchel along with you, pick up the promising rocks and drop them in your bag for proper inspection and processing later.

Once back at your camp, you can sift through the rocks you've collected, cutting and inspecting them, perhaps finding small diamonds which are somewhat plain on their own, but complement each other nicely once set into a ring together. Sometimes you'll find a truly amazing stone under the gritty outer layer, with just a little refinement and polishing required to uncover a valuable gem.

Trawling your mind for ideas is like searching for diamonds. It's something you should be doing all the time, taking along your figurative satchel so that you can drop each stone in when you happen to find it. In practice this means a notes app in your phone, or a moleskin notebook, or a steady supply of napkins and envelopes. Every time you have an idea—even the incomplete and unrefined ones—you jot it down for collection now, to be inspected and polished later. The habit of taking your idea-recording system with you *at all times* is a must-have for a world class presenter.

You can collect ideas from anywhere. Books, newspapers, magazines, conversations, day dreams, actual dreams, you name it. Anything that piques your interest is worth noting down. Especially in this day-and-age of smartphone ubiquity and applications like Evernote, there's really no compelling reasons *not* to jot down basically everything that you find interesting or potentially useful. The first step to building an ideas bank of great IP is making sure that you're capturing every good idea that you come in contact with.

Start with quotes

In 1124 Bernard Carnotensis said "Nanos gigantium humeris insidentes". Centuries later, Isaac Newton modernised the meme, saying, "If I have seen further than others, it's because I have stood on the shoulders of giants".

Their point; there is no shame in building your expertise on the prior work of others. When trying to expand and unpack your intellectual property you can use quotes to kick start your thinking. 18th century German philosopher, Johann Wolfgang von Goethe once said; "Seldom should we let the urgent take the place of the important but oftentimes we do". With that as a basis, Dr Stephen Covey went on to write *First Things First*, and built a thought leadership empire.

Famous quotes—statements of such profundity that they last through the ages—are great mental stimulators and with the advent of the internet it's easier than ever to utilise them. Identify a contextual word that encompasses some of your thinking, a word like *leverage* or *success* or *leadership* (or whatever applies in your case), and simply Google 'quotes on <your word>'. There are hundreds of sites that collect thought provoking quotations from all over the world, and these can often form the basis of excellent trains of thought.

"Yes *and…*", and "Yes *but…*"

Nobody is brilliant in a vacuum. All of the world's great thinkers have built on the foundations of ideas established by those that went before them, and you will be no exception. Fear of accusations of plagiarism is one reason people seem a little more reticent to refer to the work of others, and we strongly advocate for knocking that idea on the head. Nearly every great human advancement came about when multiple great minds tackled a problem and worked with (and sometimes against) each other, with the whole becoming more effective than the sum of the parts. Respectful attribution is the key to handling this elegantly. Always be completely open about where an idea came from, and honour the original thinker. When an audience hears a speaker praise another person in public, they appreciate a person who is willing to recognise the achievements of others. In elevating others, you elevate yourself.

So, here's a useful process for developing expertise, starting with the existing knowledge base in your field. Firstly, buy ten books on your chosen area of expertise and read them with your preferred note taking device at hand. Each time you feel compelled to write down a point made by the author, write the point and then "Yes, but…" or "Yes, and…". You're going to start with their idea, and expand it a step further.

A student says "That's a great idea".

A teacher says "That's a great idea, how do I share that?"

A leader says "That's a great idea, what do I think about that?"

The "yes, but… / yes, and…" exercise helps you build your own unique expertise upon the existing bank of ideas that exist in your field. It helps ensure you don't pigeon-hole yourself as a "me too" expert, and enables you to contribute your own unique thinking to the world. As you read each book see if you can take the disparate bits and pieces you've noted in your journal to form an overarching context. Can you identify the contextual, thematic elements that tie all this thinking together? Most authors, like most leaders, dwell in content, and your contribution to the field might be to pull all of it together into an elegant contextual whole.

Make it a mantra

A great idea can be expressed as a short, punchy statement. A slogan. The word mantra has Hindu origins, the literal meaning is "chanted or sung as an incantation or prayer", although in this context we're using it to describe the slogan you might use multiple times throughout your presentation as the punctuation of your major point. We're not suggesting you get people literally chanting your key ideas, but it is the effect we are going for.

A great speaker creates memorable phrasing. It's almost as if they are providing the language people can then use to express the ideas discussed in the presentation. It happens in conferences from time to time; when a speaker leaves such an indelible impression that for days afterwards people are using phrases from the speech. This is not just a self-rewarding goal, it's indicative that your speech has touched and influenced the audience in a positive way. You have made sense of their world and provided a frame of reference that is so agreeable that the audience chooses to carry it forward for you.

They become advocates of your leadership, and in each utterance and use of the language from your speech the size of your audience grows beyond those who were in the room when you spoke. This is the basis of a powerful meme that will grow and influence the world in a way you could never hope to on your own. As a leader you curate and create the culture of your organisation. When you hear your teams using your phrasing and language you know your message is landing.

Make it poetic

You mantra has to really capture the imagination of your audience. It becomes your catchphrase, the thing you are most associated with. You want to agonise over the wording to make it *perfect*. If your presentation is a pop song, the mantra is the chorus.

Use it repeatedly

The mantra needs to be the punctuation of your major point, and it needs to land effectively a number of times in your presentation. By the end, just as they could anticipate the chorus of a pop song on the radio, the audience should be anticipating your mantra each time you revisit your main point. They may not say it aloud, but you want them 'singing along' in their heads.

Learn from others

A number of the orators we refer to in this book have used mantras extremely effectively. Dr Martin Luther King used "I have a dream". President Obama made his mantra; "Yes we can". Totally congruent with his big word—*hope*—"yes we can" was the punctuation of many of his speeches advocating for change. Simon Sinek would often repeat "people don't buy what you do, they buy why you do it" ten or fifteen times in every presentation he gave after he released his bestseller *Start with Why*.

Building your personal idea bank is a critical step in expanding your speakership capability. Imagine the confidence that comes from having elegantly crafted messages that are fully explored and articulated to meet the needs of everyone in your audience. Imagine what you might achieve in your organisation and your career when you turn those pink sheets into a coherent set of ideas and themes that inspire action.

Cut and Polish

As your idea bank fills up with ideas and you flesh them out into pink sheets you'll need to cut and polish the ideas to turn them into diamonds. It's also time to throw away the ones you realise are just coal. "Murder your darlings" is an old piece of advice Arthur Quiller-Couch gave to aspiring writers at Cambridge University in 1914 to prevent them from the excesses of 'extraneous ornament.' It's apt to remember as you ruthlessly cut and polish your ideas, always keeping in mind what it is that most needs to be said and giving consideration to how best express the concept.

PRINCIPLE 3

Design time capsules

Anyone who went to school in the late 70's early 80's probably created and buried a time capsule for future generations to discover. Inspired by the Voyager space mission of 1977 we buried boxes that captured the prevailing mood of the time, what the Germans would call the 'Zeitgeist'. The phonograph records known as the *Voyager Golden Records* contain sounds and images meant to portray the diversity of life and culture on earth. They are a generation's stories and artifacts, built in the expectation that some future human group or maybe an extraterrestrial intelligent life might discover them. The late great Carl Sagan said that "While the chances of people discovering them are remote, the launching of this 'bottle' into the cosmic ocean says something very hopeful about life on this planet".

We now need to take each of your ideas, and design time capsules around them. Self-contained modules or packages that include stories, facts, and images that support a deeper understanding of the points you are making. These experiences need to elicit an emotional connection; an awareness of each point's identity. They serve to bring the essence of an idea or point alive in the minds of the audience.

If you recall the pink sheet framework from *Principle 2: Unpack your genius* you can see how these time capsules will mostly be composed of the content from the bottom third of the pink sheet; the stuff you use to bring each idea alive.

Study	CONTENT	Story
_____		_____
_____		_____
_____		_____
_____		_____
_____		_____

PINK SHEET   thought leaders

Each point you wish to make in a speech has its own time capsule. This is your supporting material for each idea, the talking points for each concept. They're called time capsules because they can expand and contract based on the time you have available, the purpose of the presentation, and the reception of the audience. When it's only a supporting point or the audience is catching on quickly, the time capsule can be small. When it's the central point of the presentation or the audience clearly isn't grasping it yet, the time capsule expands.

Time capsules give your presentations enormous flexibility. They give you the capacity to present a fluid and dynamic presentation tailored to the individuals in the room, and their collective mood.

Each capsule is created from the list of key concepts from the back of the envelope exercise. Your brief here in this third principle is to connect people with these ideas. If you're to capture their attention and inspire them to action, you need to make your point engaging, relevant and meaningful.

There are two pretty sexy ways to create your capsules...(drum roll please)...Excel spread sheets, or Powerpoint slide decks. What's that? They don't inspire you? Who doesn't love a good spread sheet or Powerpoint presentation? Turns out most of us. But hide your disdain for a moment, for as tools they will do a commendable job of capturing your ideas. That doesn't mean you need to present from them, but they will help organise and catalogue your thoughts perfectly. They're tools we almost universally understand and have access to; we simply need to tweak how they are used.

THE SLIDE DECK APPROACH

Probably the easiest way to design your time capsules is to create a slide deck for each point. That's one slide deck per point, but lots of slides in each deck. These can then be stored as content modules in a folder you might name IP, Concepts or Talking Points. Some will be well developed while others will be in an embryonic stage. These files then are mini slide decks that can be expanded or collapsed by hiding or showing certain slides, depending on the time you wish to allocate to each point in your final presentation. You continue to build them out over time, those you use a lot will have more slides in them, those you hardly ever touch might only have one or two slides.

What we like about this approach, if you choose to use slides when you present, is that you have done your thinking in a format that you can then use for delivery. But let's be clear that some of these slides are for you only. Some slides should never be shown to the audience.

Slides are not for bullet points. If you find yourself preparing bullet points on slides then you are scripting a speech. There is nothing wrong with this per se, but the audience should never see or know your script, right? You don't go to the movies and watch the script, you lose yourself in the experience. Audiences need to be engaged in a similar way. Having them read your speech as you are saying it is not going to make that happen.

In the speakership game we call it 'death by Powerpoint' and it's not OK, not ever, not a little bit, not even occasionally. We mean *never*!

With that off our chests, we admit Powerpoint is a great way to organise your thoughts. But if you have slides with 5 or more bullet points on them, they should be printed and used as your presenter script. What you show the audience is a completely different slide deck, a visually compelling one. One large contextual image is perfect; bullet points less so.

It's not about the slides by the way, you can still deliver these time capsules in an unplugged fashion, projector free. The slide deck is then your archive or filing system. To present unplugged simply takes a bit more preparation and understanding of your content. For most (read 98.5% of leaders) a slide deck with image based slides will free you up to deliver an awesome presentation rather than trying to recall the next example on your 4th point 38 minutes into the talk.

THE SPREADSHEET APPROACH

For most people, reading a speech is not the key to being world-class. Even though Barack Obama and other heads of state speak to the audience through transparent auto-cue glass, they know the speech off by heart. Their words can have a direct impact on world peace and the stability of global financial markets, and for this reason an auto-cue is a sensible insurance policy. They are not using the auto-cue to 'remember' their speech.

If you typically write and then read a long hand speech, then the idea of a 'cheat sheet' with your key talking points could be the solution. It will set you free from the formality of a written speech yet give you almost all of the security that a script might.

The idea of a cheat sheet for talking points is really quite simple; in essence you are creating a spreadsheet with columns and rows. Each row is for each of your key points and each column is for a variable that you might use. That would be your three to nine key points, summarised on one sheet of paper that you can refer to at a glance.

	Left Brain	Right Brain	Question	Quote
Speakership is leadership, and every tribe needs a leader	Speakership is the new leadership imperative	Speakership is the art of oration and the science of influence	Do you need to inspire your team?	Every time you speak in public, you're auditioning for a leadership position
[Point 2]	[Left brain 2]	[Right brain 2]	[Question 2]	[Quote 2]
[Point 3]	[Left brain 3]	[Right brain 3]	[Question 3]	[Quote 3]

As you can see in the example, the first column is generally dedicated to simply articulating the point. This will often be the 'A' statement from your Pink Sheet on the topic. The goal of the other columns is to build upon and reinforce the idea using 'repetitive variety'. You use as many different ways of articulating the point as necessary to give everyone in the audience a chance to absorb and comprehend the message.

You can consciously expand and contract the time capsule for each point based on the engagement and response from the audience. When you can see they're catching on quickly, you'll only use a couple of the cells in that row. When it's a more complicated point or they're struggling to understand, you might end up using all of the different versions you've prepared.

What you place in the columns is entirely up to you. You might have columns for *Left Brain* and *Right Brain* statements, or the *7/17/37/70* statements. It's a good idea to include a quote or reference from a famous thinker or philosopher who supports your idea, as well as some rhetorical questions which will get the audience thinking about the topic and how it applies to them.

You can add as many columns to this matrix as you like, limited only by the readability when printing it out. We often add columns such as references (books), metaphors, personal examples, and historical stories.

Once you've organised your main points and created all of these variations you can print them out and place them on a rostrum or lectern as your 'at a glance' reference notes. As a speaker, you then have the security of all your key ideas in front of you should you lose your way, but without losing the flexibility to deliver them in a non-scripted, relaxed, and fluid fashion. You could jump from making a point to asking a question, introducing an academic reference, and then summarising it in a casual palette.

Your second point could be introduced as a phrase, moved onto a metaphor with a historical example, and concluded by making the point in its simplest form. In this way, the audience gets to hear your key ideas in a way that looks relaxed and spontaneous, but that is, in fact, wholly premeditated.

A 'cheat sheet' with key talking points will set you free and put you on a path to delivering world-class presentations without having to rehearse your life away.

Most people, when faced with a 20-minute speech do some well-meaning but ineffective maths. They divide the time by the points and evenly distribute allocation in the speech to each point. The maths is something like '20 minutes, 10 points, that's 2 minutes a point'. This creates a boring and predictable speech that has the audience counting down your points as you go.

A far more compelling method is to build time capsules around each of your points and expand and contract them on the fly. It allows you to engage with the audience more naturally and build rapport as you speak. They'll appreciate you moving quickly through the content they 'get', and providing additional time and clarity to the points that take a bit more effort to understand.

Not all your ideas deserve the same amount of airplay at every event, and the time capsule strategy is the key to delivering messages that matter in a manner that both informs and inspires.

THE DIFFERENT TYPES OF TIME CAPSULES

We have three main types of capsules. (There are actually others but these are the best to begin with).

- Framing Capsules

- Content Capsules

- End capsules

These time capsules will be 3–18 minutes long and should be expanded or collapsed as time allows and the audience requires. Let's say you have prepared a one hour presentation, you rock up all good-to-go and the organiser says; "Jeff, you are such a star, can you get us back on time, maybe deliver your key ideas in say 30 minutes instead of an hour?". It's not really a question is it? So what do you do?

Do you talk faster and try to get through your content, complaining all way that your time got cut? Definitely not. The audience don't care about the admin and logistics. Accept that shifting time expectations is part of the game and prepare to shine no matter the time allocation.

Framing Capsules

Your framing capsule is your opening remarks. Each speech needs a series of messages that frame up the talk, letting people know what you are talking about, why it's important, and what they can hope to achieve by listening. You are going to pull ideas from your 'Inspiration drawer' created in *Principle 2 – Unpack your genius* for these framing capsules.

Each speech will need to answer some key questions right at the beginning. These are the questions on the mind of your audience, quite often subconscious questions, that block the audience hearing your message.

A number of these 15 critical questions need to be answered before the audience will hear your primary message. You want to be able to answer some, if not all, of these depending on the length of your speech.

Successfully answering these questions will leave the audience open and receptive to your message, giving you the best chance of both capturing and maintaining their attention.

BIG WORD

PRIORITY	POSITIONING	BARRIERS	SWITCHES	ACTIONS
Why you? CREDIBILITY	Why should I care? BENEFIT	What's wrong with topic? MESSAGE	What's in it for me? INTRAPERSONAL	So what should I do? PRESCRIPTION
Why now? URGENCY	What do you do? PROCESS	What's wrong with me? AUDIENCE	What's it about? EXISTENTIAL	How is it unique? DIFFERENTIATION
Why this? IMPORTANCE	Who are you? DISCLOSURE	What's wrong with you? PERSONAL	What's it like? ABSTRACT	What's your point? IMPORTANCE

Questions 1–3: Priority

The first set of questions are about making your message a priority for the audience. They help convince busy, distracted people with lots on their mind to pay attention to your message.

1. Why this message?

Given the staggering amount of information we're exposed to every day, audiences are quite selective with their attention. Just because you're on stage doesn't mean they'll listen. The amount of information we can be exposed to is staggering. A recent newspaper article suggested that 3500 books are being written every day, a mind blowing thought. The question is not "How will I find time to read them all?" but rather, "Which ones are worth my attention?". The audience needs to know why your message matters to them.

2. Why this message now?

Poll almost any audience you will ever address, and they will all report having a lot on their plate, nearly all of it highly important. This battle for priority is something you need to navigate every time you are attempting to gather people's attention around your idea or cause. They must be inspired to afford it a sense of urgency in their own work or lives.

3. Why are you the person to tell me?

In answering this question you begin to build credibility around both who you are and your message. This is where you demonstrate the depth of your history and experience. When presenting to an audience where most people know who you are you can afford some brevity here. At other times, you may need to do a full length version of your answer to the question "Why you?".

Questions 4–6: Positioning

These questions are all about positioning who you are and what you do. Assuming you have the attention of your audience, you need to then establish your credibility with them. This is about letting them know a little about who you are, what you do and why it's relevant to them and their goals.

4. Who are you?

The critical thing whenever you talk about yourself as a leader is to do so humbly. Be sure to own your success, but be quick to share how you have learnt from mistakes and failures. Bono introduced his band through career analogies; The Edge was the CTO, Adam Clayton was CFO, Larry Mullen the Head of HR and Bono himself as the plumber – because he has to clean up the stuff that goes wrong. This self-effacing positioning is a great example of talking about yourself without talking yourself up.

5. What do you do?

Explain your expertise in a simple and accesible manner. In the process, be sure to elevate others. You might recognise your good fortune in the contribution of the other smart people in your team or industry. You can say something like "I get all the credit but they do all the work". Then proceed to explain how person X's genius allows you to get Y done better than others.

6. Why should I care?

Link what you know to what people want. Explain how your solution was designed to fix three known problems the audience would readily admit. If you can articulate how what you know will help the audience get what they want—addressing their real challenges—they will feel like you are speaking directly to them. This is how you ensure you are relevant, and it is crucial. You can skip over questions four and five when pressed for time, but this one must be answered nearly every time you speak.

Questions 7–9: Barriers

These questions are all about knocking down barriers and subconscious objections. Be careful not to allow your personal insecurities, nor common generalisations of the audience, to skew your perspective on these questions.

7. What's wrong with you?

There is nothing wrong with you at all. But, at some time in your life, you will be the odd one out. Maybe you're short, or old, or bald; maybe you are white and the audience is not. Our friend and card-carrying speakership master WC Mitchell was horribly burned twice in his life. He uses a wheelchair and speaks about overcoming adversity. Seriously qualified, right? When he rolls out onto stage he immediately makes an ice-breaking joke about how he looks so that you don't feel sorry for him. His audiences immediately let go of the shock of seeing him for the first time.

Be careful that you don't come from insecurity when framing out a what's-wrong-with-you concern. Don't bring a problem into the room that doesn't exist.

8. What's wrong with them?

Everyone is prone to biases. In answering this question, you're seeking to identify and call out a bias that blocks your message. This is dangerous territory because if done in the wrong way it can lead to accusations of bigotry and flawed assumptions. There's really no return from that mistake, so tread carefully.

In considering your audience, do they exhibit a professional bias of some sort? Engineers over-specify things, which may get in the way of your message around minimum viable product and the need to launch faster. Accountants over-analyse things, which might make them hesitant to take more entrepreneurial risks.

The trick is to frame the audience's bias in a complimentary way and position the disruption or change that is instructing your thinking. Ask for their thoughts, and then position your message.

9. What's wrong with your message?

If you know your message is a hard pill to swallow, it's useful to acknowledge that publicly. Perhaps it's expensive, or time consuming, or challenging, or simply a long way removed from the existing paradigm. The cynics in the room want to resist change, and you need to demonstrate that you understand how your solution works in the real world.

Often you can lay out past thinking, current thinking, and future thinking in such a way that the message that is in your speech is the current thinking, and the actual present thinking is old and in the past.

By creating a third space, the future thinking, bigger than your idea, you are showing that your idea represents a cautious evolution to new thinking rather than a revolutionary leap from their existing world view.

Questions 10–12: Switches

The fourth set of questions engage the smart cookies to your message. Howard Gardner (Harvard learning specialist) identified three major listening modes or switches that people choose when they are already reasonably familiar with your topic. These will need to be addressed particularly when your audience members think they know a lot about your topic.

The three switches need to be addressed pretty early in your presentation. Fail to address these and you risk the possibility that the smarter members of the audience 'white ant' you, undermining your message and eroding your credibility.

10. What's it like?

This question addresses the need for referencing. Either literal references as in 'I read this book and it got me thinking', or some kind of reference to a past experience, such as 'Do you guys remember when Jonnie from accounts spoke at the 2012 conference?', or even using metaphors and analogies. Referencing helps people to see that you are not passing off other people's ideas as your own. Quote others, hold up books, make references or describe shared experiences, and use analogies to start your conversation.

11. What's it about?

This question positions your message into a primary overarching context. This is your big word from the top of the pink sheet. Build a memorable phrase that anchors that word in a way that's easy to recall. This helps meta-thinkers and people who are across the detail of what you are talking about find a way to engage with your angle. It's like a folder in their brain opens up and all their existing knowledge and understanding becomes easily accessible. They'll grasp your message much earlier in the presentation and be much more likely to support your agenda.

12. What's in it for me?

The 'me' in this case may be 'my group' or 'my division' or 'my family', and it's not an unreasonable question for someone to ask. So many people are pushing their agendas that it's hard to separate the good from the bad. Take time to get really clear for your audience about what the pay-off is for them. Simply stack at least three reasonable and realistic benefits, skills and positive outcomes that the audience can expect from your proposal.

Questions 13–15: Action

The last three questions are about action and driving change. Leaders drive results and these three last questions are a result of all your previous hard work on the 12 previous questions.

13. What's your point?

By this time in the framing process we are ready to start delivering key ideas. Make sure that your point is clear and well-articulated. These are your concept statements from the middle of the pink sheet, and the key is to utilise repetitive variety. You want to use a number of different phrases and statements reinforcing the same point, whether they be left-brain/right-brain, 7/17/37/70, or whichever method you chose to create your points.

Repetitive variety gives the everyone in the audience a chance to lock into your message and understand it deeply.

14. How is it unique?

Make sure you can explain how your idea is unique; look for a point of difference. The easiest point of difference is to be a contrarian. Pick a sacred cow or an established thought and challenge it. We like to call this "throwing rocks". A similar strategy is to target an enemy to your idea and place your key message in counterpoint to a well-established concept.

Another strategy is to show how you've taken two existing ideas and intersected them in a unique way.

15. So what should I do?

Our final frame is the action frame. Once the audience is convinced of both the urgency and importance of your message, you need to provide the way forward. What actions can they take away? Give them a thinking exercise, or three steps they can implement tomorrow. Make them practical as well as conceptual.

The 15 questions are a great thinking process designed to help you construct your framing time capsules. As always, be prepared to expand and contract what you say based on the time allocated. A framing capsule would typically be anywhere from 3–18 minutes long.

We reckon there's four groups of these questions that you want to answer, depending on the length of your speech.

- If you're working in *extremely* limited time, just answer the first three in one short, punchy statement.

- If your speech is a short 20-minute presentation then answer 1, 2, 11, 12, 13 and 15. These six questions can be answered in a five minute framing piece, and will give you a fantastic foundation on which to build a compelling message.

- If you had 45 minutes to an hour to speak, you might also try to answer 6, 9, 10 and 14. Answering these questions helps you cut through the information overload and flag your idea as relevant and important.

- If you are speaking for 90 minutes or longer then you would probably attempt to deal with all 15 questions. The majority of the questions would be built into your framing capsule, with the rest peppered throughout the speech.

Every minute spent in framing makes every other minute in your speech vastly more effective. No matter what, no matter how much time pressure you have, no matter how often you have done the talk; always, always, always spend some time on framing.

Content Capsules

You have now spent at least a third of your speaking time on the framing, we know what you are thinking: "There is no time left for my message!". Just because you're onstage doesn't mean you have their attention, and just because you're talking doesn't mean they're listening. The framing capsules set up the audience to get your points, to really listen. Without good framing you are wasting their time and yours.

With the foundation set, it's time to deliver some content. Using the slide deck method for designing time capsules, you might build a slide deck per point that looks like this (remember this is for one point).

Slide	Summary
1 Concept	This brightly coloured slide is hidden from the audience, and is used to mark the beginning of each time capsule in the presenter view.
2 Mantra	Embed your key mantra on a nice contextual image.
3 Statistics stack	A set of data that provides the empirical evidence to validate your idea.
4 Infographic	Bring the data to life visually with an infographic that makes it easy for the more creative types to digest, and further reinforces your point.
5 Book cover	Display a great book on the topic (whether a classic, contemporary, or current best seller) and describe the key points. Read the book first!
6 Famous person (living)	Describe how this famous person supports or embodies the message. Include imagery of them that supports the idea.
7 Quote	Display a quote from a respected authority on the topic. Share something we may not know about the person and their story.
8 University campus	Discuss a piece of academic research on the topic with this slide as a backdrop.
9 Case study	Discuss an example of your idea in action with an appropriate supporting image of the people/place on screen.
10 Story	Pick an evocative image to display that adds drama to your story.
11 Model	Display the model from your Pink Sheet. You wouldn't often use this slide. It's generally better to 'build' the model with your body as you talk.
12 Interview	With longer presentations (or smaller audiences) you may use accompanying video footage of a relevant interview or biography.

If you're committing only a couple of minutes to the first point, you might use only slides 1, 2 and 9. Perhaps the second point is the key message of your presentation so you use all the slides from that capsule. Point three, you might mix it up and use slides 1, 2, 4, 6, 9 and 10.

Your time capsules are a collection of stories, pictures, and ideas that serve to bring your key topic points to life. Collapse and expand each capsule and you get to deliver the same key idea, but with varying degrees of illustration.

Closing Capsules

You have framed up the topic and delivered some brilliant content to illustrate your points, it's now time to bring it home. The closing capsules are your chance to reinforce key messages, focus the audience's attention and more than anything, make a difference to the human condition.

Three things you might want to include in your closing remarks:

1. A quick summary of what you have said.

2. Some prescriptive 'do this' calls to action

3. A statement or two about desire, belief, focus, commitment and action. These five 'motivation' themes have been shown to illicit a positive response from a crowd.

If nothing changes when you sit down after a presentation, what was the point? Influence is your agenda; giving people motivation (a motive for action) is your role. Unfortunately, many leaders seem to think informing is the goal. In this era of seemingly unlimited knowledge, it's not. A report can inform, a video can inform, a simple email could inform. The opportunity cost of bringing a room full of people together is far too great to simply inform.

Your job is to inspire.

PUTTING IT ALL TOGETHER

Now that you have some framing ideas, content ideas and closing ideas you then prepare your presentation by grabbing 3, 5 or 7 of these time capsules into a speech file that you name based on the event and/or date of the presentation.

As a rough rule of thumb:

- A 20-minute presentation is 3 content capsules (points)

- A 60-minute presentation is 5 content capsules

- A 90-minute presentation is 7 content capsules

Visually it might look like this:

PRINCIPLE 4

Amplify your self

Audiences aren't looking for the same carbon-copy speaker they've seen a thousand times before. They're looking for authenticity. They're looking for speakers who really believe what they're saying and deliver their message with honesty and integrity. From Sir Ken Robinson, who delivers his speech while hardly moving from the spot; to Hans Rosling who is almost literally climbing the walls by the time he gets to the climax of his presentation; everyone has their own style, because everyone is unique. No-one is 'youer' than you.

When you move from the preparation of the content of your speech to the live delivery you're forced to confront the fear of self-exposure. The fact that everyone is staring at you with great expectation creates a game of hide and seek. You're seeking to engage with the audience, and yet you tend to hide the parts of yourself that are the most interesting.

There are a few contributing factors here:

- You are only on stage for a short while, so it's difficult to get 'warmed up'.

- All the attention is on you, and the normal give-and-take of conversation is missing.

- You worry that you're uninteresting; a basic confidence issue.

- Humility teaches us to focus less on ourselves than on others.

- You endeavour to be something you imagine the audience wants you to be, rather than being who you are.

Being yourself while presenting can be a real challenge. The paradox of public speaking is: you can't just be yourself; you need to amplify yourself. You have to not only be yourself, but a really *great* version of yourself. An 'er' version. Louder, larger, bigger, funnier, goofier, brainier, clumsier, wiser. A 'more' version. More entertaining, more articulate, more judgmental, more forthright. Whatever the 'you' of you is, we need to see that on stage—amplified. Before your audience will buy what you say, they're buying who you are.

It's a mistake to think that great performances and charisma come from putting on personas and 'faking it til you make it'. In fact, authenticity and genuine connection come from taking your masks off. Brene Brown's ground-breaking work on vulnerability goes to the heart of this dilemma.

You need to bring all facets of your personality to the stage. Tell an embarrassing story (strategically), share a skeleton (that aligns with your message); be open and accessible. You, by being publicly okay with all the different parts of who *you* are, send a message to the audience that you are okay with all the different parts of who *they* are. People feel comfortable around people who feel comfortable. As the leader, you need to be comfortable with yourself at the front of the room. Comfortable with your strengths, and more importantly comfortable with your weaknesses. Your audience wants to feel like they're in safe hands. That confidence isn't engendered when you big note and talk yourself up. It comes when they see your humanity, the whole of you. An audience that feels safe and accepted, and trusts the leader at the front of the room, is an audience ready to be influenced

IDENTIFYING UNIQUENESS

You are one of a kind! You know this already. To develop the most compelling version of yourself for the stage you need to understand which aspects of your uniqueness to amplify. What can you use in service of your message?

Your natural instinct might be to focus in on things you are really good at. Resist! Often the things that make you most 'you' to other people are the flaws, the idiosyncrasies, the imperfections.

To discover your compelling uniqueness, look no further than your faults.

Step 1: Identify your greatest weakness

You might think that having a wild imagination and dreaming up fanciful stories of adventuring children in magical lands would not be a particularly practical trait to be blessed with, and yet JK Rowling managed to channel this ability into something incredibly productive and meaningful. You might assume that perfectionism so crippling it prevents you from buying any furniture and leaves you literally sitting on the floor of your living room for years would be a terrible burden, and yet Steve Jobs used it to develop products like the iPad and iPhone. As a speaker you need to identity your greatest weakness and use it to enhance your audience's understanding of who you are.

What do you get wrong? What is a recurring theme in your life? What challenges do you keep butting your head up against? In your relationships with others, what do they say you need to work on? What's that part of your personality that makes people groan, slap their forehead and say "That's just classic <your name>" whenever it comes out? You'll know you've found the right one when it makes you a bit uncomfortable to even admit it to yourself.

Step 2: Anchor the opposite of this weakness

What is the opposite of your answer? Not the antonym, necessarily, but the antidote. If someone was fed up with you and your trait, they might tell you "Do this" or "Become this" or "You need to develop more of this". They might have told J.K. Rowling to be more down to earth, to get a normal job and concentrate on reality for once. They might have told Steve Jobs to be more easy-going and accept that 'good' is 'good enough'. Once you identify the opposite of your trait, we want you to note it down for reference and then *completely ignore it*. You're not to be lured into the 'work on your weaknesses' line. To expand your uniqueness you need to live in your strengths! It's about standing out not fitting in.

Step 3: Flip the negative and make it a positive

Take your answer from step one, and flip it into a positive. J.K. Rowling is not a dreamer, she's incredibly creative. Steve Jobs was not a perfectionist, he was a visionary. Take your supposedly negative character trait, and flip it into your uniqueness.

If the negative is...	Then the positive spin is
I over-commit	I'm passionate
I'm judgemental	I'm discerning
I'm too direct	I'm honest
I'm stubborn	I have strength of conviction

Being passionate might not feel unique. There are surely a lot of passionate people in the world. But only you are passionate in the way that you are passionate. Bestselling author Elizabeth Gilbert puts it like this: "The older I get, the less I care about originality, because it can feel forced and artificial. What I love, though, is authenticity, because it's rare."

Comedians absolutely revel in this game. Almost every comedian in the world will take their supposedly negative character flaws and flip them into their unique stage identity, their signature style. Every overweight comedian absolutely *owns* their body shape. The nerdy guy will always ham up the awkwardness. The shrieking mother will wail like a banshee on stage.

Your compelling uniqueness lies not in your strengths, but your imperfections. As we work through the other tools and skills of the *Method* to bring your *Message* alive, look for opportunities to tap into your uniqueness and ways to let it be seen in your presentations.

THE PERSONA PROJECT

The persona project is one tool we have to amplify authenticity and amplify your self on stage. It helps create humour and drama, and brings a great deal of personality and life to your presentations. In short, it's the use of amplified characters—'versions of you'—which help you breathe life into the stories you tell.

A word of caution around this advice: you have to be strong in your vulnerability. While being authentic for your audience provides them with a much more fulfilling experience, you have to avoid 'therapy on stage' at all costs. Be clean, and use your disclosure in service of others, not just to satisfy some self-exploration or indulgence. If you can't share a story without losing yourself in the emotion of what happened, you're not ready to tell that story. Look at the way comedians use their personal quirks as a vehicle for communication. Whether they be fat, or short, or introverted, or neurotic; whatever shortcomings are revealed to the audience it's never done for pity, it's to engineer a more rapid human connection.

The persona project is a practical, step-by-step guide for identifying those parts of yourself that you typically hide around strangers. This will (seemingly paradoxically) make you a much more powerful and memorable speaker when you deliver an amplified version of these parts of yourself to the audience in your presentation.

Step 1. Identify 6–12 characters that express who you are in different context

Take a piece of paper and map out some compartments of your personality or life, often the sides of yourself that you keep hidden from view most of the time. Maybe they're a bit extreme, or maybe you're not quite so proud of some of them! Give them silly names so you can objectify the trait and examine it without getting too caught up in yourself.

Some examples we've seen before include: Crazy Stalker Girl, Mad Professor, Boy Wonder, Bush Accountant, Jealous Boyfriend, Rockstar Wannabe, Princess Perfect, Florence the Rescuer, Westy Bogan, Skater Boy, Fantasy Freak, Whirling Dervish.

Get creative! Dive into yourself and release all of the freaks and misfits that you hide day-to-day. It can be fun to identify and then embrace parts of yourself that you usually hide, or only bring out with certain friends and situations. It can be quite a healing process to discover those parts of you that you hide most of the time, and acknowledge them as being okay, and for you to be okay with them as part of you.

This approach is not part of some new age personal development program. This is a practical strategy for making you a more effective presenter. It will help you deliver your message with greater engagement and authenticity. As a leader it reveals more of you to your team in a way that connects them to your message. Taken too seriously or indulged in the wrong way, the persona project could become a negative influence. Stay light and somewhat flippant as you play with your various personas.

Step 2. Tap into these characters to make your presentations more appealing

Three ways you might do this:

1. Find a metaphor or analogy out of the character that serves you when you speak.

2. Adopt some movement or dramatisation from the stereotyping of the different characters.

3. Explore stories or narrative from each of these personas and characters.

Want to deliver a story about poor customer service? It'll be much more powerful if you call on *Bored Teenager* (the disinterested kid you used to be) in order to really demonstrate the disdain of the disengaged customer service representative.

Want to rant about the so-called leaders in management who are entirely focused on themselves? It'll be much more memorable if you engage your *Inner Rockstar* as you assume the role of the self-absorbed, destructive middle-manager who is costing the company thousands in poor morale.

Trying to convince the company to make a bold decision and take a risk? Bring forth the *Intrepid Adventurer* to describe the dangers of the journey and the benefits that lie beyond in the promised land.

Another way to access different personas is to think about your different roles and hobbies. Are you a frustrated musician? A devoted childless uncle? An enthusiastic foreign film buff? Think about each of these versions of you might bring life and energy to your speeches. Gihan Perera plays the piano on stage, but in keeping with his message around technology he uses an iPad to do so. Playing a clip from a movie you love that aids your message also lets your audience see more of who you are. All of this *Method* serves your message by making it more engaging and memorable for your audience.

SIGNATURE STYLES

Develop a signature style which declares to the audience who you are and what you're about. People are quick to pass judgement and if you don't send a clear signal, your audience will make assumptions, flattering or otherwise.

When it comes to developing a signature brand or style, you need to take charge of the various ways in which you are being perceived by others.

We don't have to look far to find abundant examples of speakers and leaders who prove that amplified authenticity through a strong signature style is a patently successful strategy.

Steve Jobs was never seen on stage without his New Balance 992's and his plain black turtleneck sweater. Combined with his obvious passion for product design and his "Insanely great" catchphrase, Jobs provided the archetype of modern product announcement. His visage became so recognisable as to become synonymous with Apple's stage, and he successfully led a tribe of millions. Do you reckon anyone in Steve's life thought his on-stage uniform was a bit 'naff'? They must have. Come on. A skivvy? It's not hard to imagine a friend or colleague trying to help him out by making fashion suggestions, is it? But to do so would have been to damage his brand and the expression of his personality on stage. What is important here—the reason to amplify your authenticity—is to help the audience identify and empathise with you in the lopsided conversation you're having with them.

Seth Godin didn't get embarrassed by his bald head and attempt to hide it. To the contrary, he made a feature of it by making just the top half of his head the cover of his magnum opus. It became an integral part of his brand and his performance. Audiences seeing Seth on stage immediately identify with his geeky, thoughtful sensibility. Malcolm Gladwell's signature afro came about when he didn't go to the hairdresser one year because he's a man not particularly concerned with fashion. Suddenly, he felt like audiences were responding to him better, as if his hair was having a bit of an Einstein effect.

There are loads of things you could do. Wear eyeglasses matching the colour of your shoes. Wear a bowtie of a different colour every time you speak, on a pressed white shirt with a pen holder. Don a lab coat with your brand embroidery. Maybe use a blackboard and chalk instead of a flipchart. Maybe you could invite guests on stage and sit on a couch with them like a talk show. The possibilities are limitless, and speakers have to 'rockstar' more than any other kind of expert. These might all sound like gimmicky affectations, but imagine if you went to an Apple product release and Steve Jobs had walked onto stage wearing a business suit. Imagine if you went to see U2 play in concert and Bono didn't wear his glasses! You would be surprised—and more likely disappointed—if any one of them turned up without, or with something other than, their signature 'bit'.

And remember, you're not trying to please everyone. There is no tribe in the world that includes everyone. People gravitate towards individuals that they identify with, and 'vanilla' is rarely what they're looking for. If no-one is criticising your signature style you probably don't have one. If you are trying to fit in, how can you possibly stand out? You have to bring as much of your personality to bear as possible in the first three minutes.

So, how do we ride the line between signature and gimmick? There's three basic rules:

1. Consistent: You want to be more comfortable in your style than in anything else. It's with you all the time, not just on stage. So if suits are not your thing, and you love the idea of jeans, then make jeans part of your style. It becomes an expression of you, as opposed to an affectation of who you'd like to be; it's congruent with who you are.

2. Congruent: It needs to be an element in a whole constellation of ideas—a whole bunch of things, not just some weird

quirky thing for the sake of it. And, for that matter, any single thing by itself is usually going to stand out as a deliberate gimmick. A few subtle touches that complement each other are much more likely to work effectively.

3. Beneficial: It adds to your message. People will accept and embrace any oddity or uniqueness if it is directed in some way to helping them. If your message is about embracing passion, and your style includes subtle leopard print touches, the audience is going to love it. If your message is about the value of attention to detail, but your shoes look worn out the audience is not going to love it. Make your style a canvas upon which the art of your message looks incredible. This is the value of a signature style, and it's why superficial is anything but.

Speakership is about spreading messages that matter. Everything we say, everything we do, everything we project contributes to how that message is heard. What you say is less important than what your audience hears, and they cannot separate the message from the messenger. So your look, your style, your character becomes an integral part of the message. It can affirm and elevate the message, or it can detract from it.

Amplifying your self is all about letting people see you, the real you, amplified in service of your message.

PRINCIPLE 5

Entertain the crowd

When you step up to address a room, whether it's a cosy group of 30 or a ballroom of 300, your presentation is never a mere oral statement of truths. It's not an essay read aloud. It's showtime!

Edutainment is the exciting mix of entertainment and education. Increasingly, university professors are enlivening their lectures with music, humourous skits, and dangerous experiments. We all remember the mad scientists who attempted to blow up the science labs in our high school chemistry classes as a means to entertain and engage us. In our fast paced hi-tech world the struggle for attention is real. The best way to keep your audience plugged into your presentation is to have a message worth hearing and a method of delivering it that directly engages their emotions.

Aristotle divided the means of persuasion into three parts: Pathos, Logos and Ethos. Logos is the use of logic to support your claims; facts, statistics and the use of solid reasoning. Ethos is your credibility, the authority on which you stand as an expert or someone worthy of any audience. And Pathos is where the power of performance resides. Using vivid language and emotional appeals through the use of sensory details, stories, anecdotes, humour and drama is a critical component of entertaining the crowd.

Make them laugh, make them think, make them care.

GET ANIMATED

Getting rockstar good at being up the front requires you to get animated. Move. Big gestures. Deliberate positioning on the stage. Your face has to light up with contrasting expressions to bring your stories, your jokes, and your case studies to life. Your voice has to show contrast and add dramatic flair to what you're saying. Every presentation you give needs to be a full-on 3D multi-sensory experience.

You can't talk earnestly about energy, passion, and courage while your feet are rooted to the spot and your arms are stuck in your pockets. If your message is about balance, calm, and mindfulness you can't be running all over the stage or pacing from side to side like a caged polar bear.

If you think about the front of the room being a theatre stage, challenge yourself to put on a decent show. If a photo was taken every 3 minutes during your presentation we'd expect that in at least some of the photos you'd have moved to use different parts of the stage.

Give yourself a reason to move your hands in the first ten seconds of your presentation. Have a scripted gesture that accompanies your introduction that gets your body moving and into a natural rhythm. Once you have some momentum, maintaining it is easy, so the key is simply to *start moving*. Once you're underway, your natural communication skills will take over. For most people, just getting their hands away from their body *once* is enough to get them into their natural rhythm. Your audience is looking at you. Give them something to look at.

THE TEE

The Tee is a way of dividing up the stage (or any space in which you are presenting) into positions that makes your message easier to understand, and easier to remember. These are two vitally important characteristics of a powerful meme so you definitely want to use this tool.

It's called the Tee because when you view the stage from above the audience you draw a letter T on it as a roadmap of where you can go.

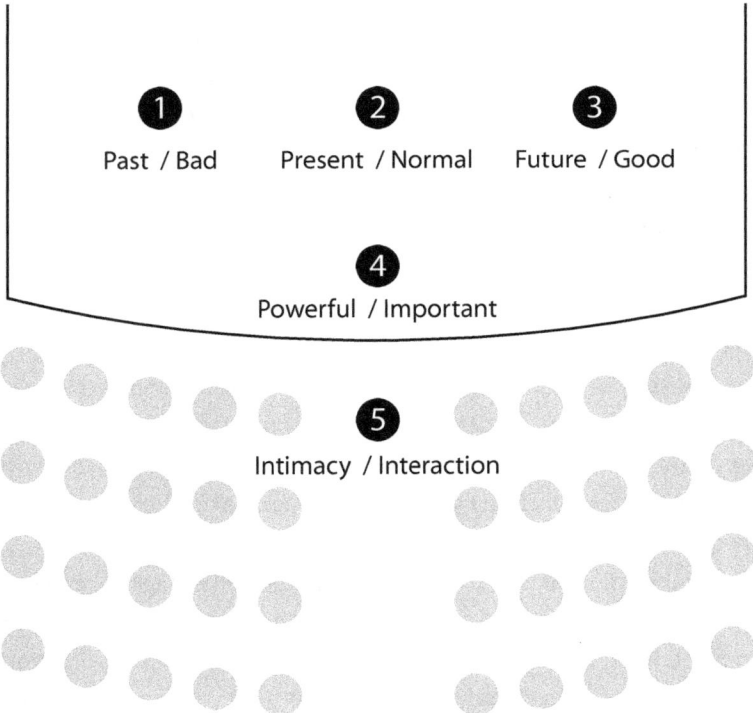

① Past / Bad   **②** Present / Normal   **③** Future / Good

④ Powerful / Important

⑤ Intimacy / Interaction

Starting with the "top row" of the Tee—positions 1, 2 and 3—what you need to do is anchor each point of your message to a location on the stage. This idea of anchoring is really important. As the presenter, you must be cognisant of your location with every point that you make, because subconsciously the audience certainly is. If you are careful to return to the same place on the stage each time you revisit a point, it helps to cement idea in the minds of the audience, making it easier to understand and easier to remember.

Humans have evolved to visually identify and remember movements and associate them with ideas very quickly. Being able to quickly identify the reaction of another tribesman to a predator, for example, has an obvious advantage where survival is concerned; and thus the brain became highly attuned to observing and remembering movements, along with their associated meanings.

Whatever the evolutionary reasons, our ability to recognise movements quickly and easily—and associate them with meaning—is of crucial importance to anyone aiming to communicate effectively in the modern world. In this book, our objective is to ensure that the movements you employ in your presentations are congruent with your points, reinforce their meaning, and help to convey them with maximum impact. This is theatre, not radio.

The key point about this type of stagecraft is consistency. Choose a place, anchor an idea there, and then return to that place every time you want to revisit the idea. It's possible to put any idea anywhere on the stage—you can effectively teach your audience where your ideas 'live'.

Position 4, right at the front in the middle of the stage, is reserved for the key point you want the audience to take home from your presentation. It's a powerful and somewhat confronting location from which to speak, and as such it's best used rarely and carefully. But it should most certainly be used to underscore the key message of your presentation.

Position 5, down the stairs and into the audience, is your opportunity to break the "fourth wall". Taken from show business, the fourth wall is a term that describes the barrier between the audience and the show. The first three walls surrounding the show are, of course, the three edges of the stage or film set. The fourth wall is the invisible barrier between the actors and the audience or the camera lens. Breaking this barrier can be surprising, but it's a great method of building rapport and creating a friendly and welcoming environment. It can help demonstrate that you consider yourself one of them, which builds likeability and trust.

In planning your 'speech on an envelope', one of your key tools should be where on the stage, in the room, or at the table you plan to be to deliver each key point. This simple piece of information will not only enhance the delivery of your speech, but it also helps you to remember the format and structure of your presentation. Your speech will have a simple 'flow', a deliberate movement through the presentation space, which provides you with a kinaesthetic means of remembering the path of your speech.

GIVING GOOD FACE

Animating your face doesn't always come easily. Part of our corporate cultural baggage is a tendency to maintain a poker face so that others we're working with can't see what we're really thinking.

Go back to your favourite comedians, and storytellers. Watch as they use their eyes, an upturn of their mouths, a radiant smile or a fierce scowl to add to their performances. Giving good face on stage is about ensuring that your facial expression matches the intensity of your message. The contrast in your presentation should be reflected by the contrast in your face.

Practising in front of a mirror won't help. There's too much simultaneous feedback. Video yourself speaking to a group and watch it back. You'll immediately see areas you can improve, as well as pick up any facial or verbal tics you have that get in the way of your message.

VOCAL GYMNASTICS

Spread a wide smile across your face. And tell the next person you see that you are very, very angry with them.

It can't be done. The emotion in your voice is so closely linked to the expression on your face. Great speakers know that their voices work best when they are on their feet, moving and grooving and giving great face. This is part of making sure that everything is aligned with their message.

The variables you need to control as you move towards mastery are pitch, pace, tone, and volume. Great speakers will alter their speed and volume deliberately to create momentum and contrast. One tone, one pace, one volume is never going to have the impact or influence you're after, and it certainly won't be entertaining.

Every time you prepare to speak, choose moments of contrast. Find the place in your talk that will be enhanced by an intimate, quieter voice. Look for an opportunity to get louder, to keep attention levels high. There might be an opportunity for a faster delivery—a list or a rant. Perhaps a moment to pause for emphasis.

Your ability to bring your speech to life through movement, gesture, facial expressions, and vocal contrast will be a key factor in your speakership success. Be a leader worth seeing live.

THE PROBLEM WITH POWERPOINT

Visual tools like slides, whiteboards and flipcharts can all be effectively used to add excitement and variety to a presentation, to make it more entertaining.

One extraordinarily common mistake is the overuse of these tools, particularly slide decks. The expression 'death by Powerpoint' survives because of its essential truth. Most Powerpoint presentations are boring, poorly designed, full of text with too many bullet points, amateur in their animation, ugly to look at, discordant with the message and over-arching context of the speech, incongruent with the big purpose of the presenter, and poorly controlled by the person giving the talk. And that's just the first few reasons we encourage speakers to err on the side of 'less is more'.

If you want to show your audience a model, a slide can only ever be a 2 dimensional version. Boring, bored, asleep. Bring your models alive by *becoming* your diagrams. Using your body and the stage as a canvas, your mission is to use gesture and position to create an imaginary 3 dimensional version of your diagram in the space around you.

Say for example you're talking your audience through a standard Venn-diagram, three circles arranged in a pyramid. As you make your first point, you can move a step to your right, and gesture subtly to the floor to your right. This becomes the bottom-left circle for the audience. Stepping and gesturing to your left for your next point, the audience sees the bottom-right circle. Finally, you can step back to the middle, look up and raise your hands to make the final point, creating the last circle of the Venn diagram in the air in front of you.

Of course, you could then talk about how those three points blend together in the middle, reaching forward with a hand to indicate the area where the three circles meet. All of this can be done very effectively without explaining to the audience that you're drawing a model, and without showing them the model on an accompanying slide. Everyone is born with the innate ability to recognise what you're doing.

It's definitely worth trying to use as much vertical space as you can. It's easy to walk around and gesture side-to-side, but this can create only a limited amount of variety. You've got arms and legs—use them! Stretch right up high with your arms, look up, gesture to an imaginary point far above you. Bend your knees, get down low, touch the floor with your hands. You have a huge amount of vertical space around you. Your diagrams—and your speech as a whole—will really come to life if you utilise the full height of your body to depict them.

USING HUMOUR

Laughter breaks down barriers faster than almost any other social interaction, and the ability to use humour to your advantage is an extremely valuable asset for any speaker. It's not a nice to have—it's an essential. To entertain the crowd at some stage of your presentation, and earlier is better, you want them to laugh.

Humour switches off people's judgemental filters and opens them up to considering your ideas. If they're laughing, they're open for learning.

Humour really is an artful science. Science, in that there are formulas and steps you can follow, and yet there is an art in the intuitive sense of timing required. Always, appropriateness is key.

Here are several ideas to help you be funnier when you speak.

Tell stories, not jokes

It's much easier to use humorous stories to lighten things up than to deliver jokes. Most jokes will definitely offend. Situational comedy is nice and safe. Seinfeld built an Emmy award-winning show based on funny situations.

Google for laughs

Jokes are risky but the punch-line often isn't. A joke usually has a setup and a punch-line. Google 'jokes on (the key topic)' or idea in your stories, and you can often weave the punch-line into your stories as an off-hand comment, rather than fully set up the joke.

Use your audience

The people in your audience are often funnier than you will ever be. If you can get comfortable with a degree of audience participation and interaction, you can often lift the mood by bouncing humour around with your audience. This technique is kind of like flirting with the humour that exists in the room. Work with what you have available to you.

If you are not naturally funny, then let them be. Over time, as you relax into this role, you may find yourself dropping small light-hearted comments into the humour provided. In this way, you can build on the work being done by the jokers in the room.

Make fun of yourself

Self-deprecation is the safest route to humour. Sarcasm is the riskiest. It's easy to poke fun at others but this is hardly ever a successful strategy for speakers. The ability to laugh at yourself is a fabulous signal that you are relaxed and not too nervous. It also shows you respect the room and are not cocky or overly confident.

THE ANCIENT CRAFT OF STORY-TELLING

All our most popular forms of entertainment are built around stories. Movies, books, video games. Even sport relies on stories to bring punters back week after week. Every entertaining presentation is punctuated by stories. Watch the 10 most popular TED talks of all time. Story, point, story, story, point, point, story. Notice how often the stories contain punchlines, small jokes that provoke a laugh, a smile. Notice how the emotionally moving stories are told to make the audience care, not cry.

Your ability to inhabit your stories, be the characters, use accents, adopt their body movements, and use the space around you on the stage will dramatically improve the memorability of your message.

Stories work because they are emotional and appeal to our senses. There are characters, tensions, hopes and dreams that all get exposed on a roller coaster journey. Joseph Campbell's 'hero's journey' storyline is a great formula, Nancy Duarte also brings this into the 21st century with her Resonance book and TED talk.

The formula for basic speech storytelling is:

1. Set the scene

2. Introduce complication

3. Create characters and build relationships

4. Resolve the complication

5. Come out on top

The case study

The simplest story structure is the case study. The data for this story is taken from among the left-brain content of your IP snapshot. Case studies are factual, with real people, names, data, statistics and results.

Anecdote Formula for Case Studies

1. Incident - this is what happened

2. Point - this is what you can conclude from that

3. Benefit - this lets us achieve X or Y

The historical story

Many presenters make the mistake of constantly telling stories about themselves. 'This one time, at band camp.' The danger of using stories about yourself is that generally the protagonist in a story is also the hero—and repeatedly talking about yourself as a hero is unlikely to work with your audience. It creates distance not commonality.

Using the pronoun 'I' in a presentation has an enormous effect on how the speaker is perceived by the audience. People tend not to warm to speakers who say "me, my, I" a lot, compared to those who say "you, they, we, us" and so making someone else the protagonist of some of your stories is a good strategy for connecting with the audience. They will appreciate your willingness to admire and elevate others.

The classic story structures have endured because they take the audience on an emotional journey. They are entertaining. Laughter, tears, apprehension, resolution. The details change, but the story remains the same. Pretty Woman is My Fair Lady. Harry Potter is Star Wars.

Brain candy

Every time you share an interesting tidbit with your audience, in a bite sized piece that ignites their curiosity or sense of wonder, you increase the likelihood of your messages being remembered and shared.

Social object theory suggest that people share photos, stories, quote, factoids as a way of connecting with each other. And what do we share? Things that entertain us.

Part of entertaining the crowd is to move beyond trivia and facts that support your messages to creating brain candy that will delight your audience.

> "Did you know that every year the number of accounting graduates in India exceeds the total number of accountants in the whole of Australia?"

If your speech is about the market for talent and disruption in professional industries such as accounting and law, this brain candy is easily shareable and likely to be remembered by your audience. You can just imagine them out for dinner the night of your talk sharing this new factoid with the table.

> "If we keep consuming energy at the current levels, the best guestimates are that by 2050—less than 35 years away—we will need 4 and a half planets the size of earth to house us all."

Pace of change, the need for fresh thinking, environmental concerns can all be illustrated with this little gem.

Talking about resilience, perseverance, rejection, self-belief? Offer a social object in the form of brain candy list. Top selling authors rejected more than 30 times by publishers? Stephen King with *Carrie*, Margaret Mitchell—*Gone with the Wind*. *Zen and the Art of Motorcycle Maintenance* was rejected 121 times before it was published. Twelve publishers turned down the first *Harry Potter* book.

The trick is to look for ways that you can nail your key messages with examples that are entertaining and shareable.

Emotion is the superhighway to learning and memorability. As a leader, your ability to connect with your audience and have them care about anything you're saying will be greatly enhanced each time your audience is entertained.

PRINCIPLE 6

Work the room

The Tonight Show with Jimmy Fallon. Ellen. Oprah. All television shows. All have long waiting lists for ticket sales. Why? Because nothing beats live. When you attend the live taping you get to be part of the audience and interact with the stars. You're part of the show in a way that's entirely different from just watching the show at home. The interaction, the feel of being part of the whole experience, is worth the price of the ticket and the length of the wait.

Brilliant leadership presentations are exactly the same. The presence of the audience makes your whole speech a co-created experience where the involvement and interaction of the audience is crucial. You job at the front is to work the room. Connect, interact, and metaphorically shake hands with everyone in the audience.

When you're committed to presenting in service of the tribe you lead, your speech must be a conversation. You'll be doing the majority of the talking, but you always want to speak from the mindset of leading a conversation rather than dictating from a script. The more meaningful interaction you have, the more likely your memes will be memorable and shared beyond the audience to the wider tribe.

Here are some tools and methods we can use in order to accomplish this goal.

I, YOU, WE

The speakership master model we presented at the beginning of the book has three layers of focus: Speaker (I), Audience (You), Tribe (We). Moving the focus of your presentation from yourself, out to the audience, and up into a conversation in service of the tribe is one of the central themes of this book.

The following structure enables you to plan your interaction with the audience in a way that gives them time to think, time to talk, and the opportunity to reach their own conclusions. The progression from speaker, to audience, to tribe creates the primary means by which we generate audience interaction, which you can remember with the mantra "I talk, you talk, we talk".

"I talk"

You're the presenter, and it starts with you talking. You set the context of the discussion, provide the data required, and leave enough space in the delivery to let the audience think about each point as it lands. Imagine yourself conversing with others at a party. When someone else is leading a conversation you're in, you're happy to listen.

However, there comes a point when you want to pipe up and add your own point of view. Even if only to affirm what they're saying, you want to have at least a bit of input every now and then to keep involved in the discussion. When presenting, your audience feels the same way! So start by talking, and giving them the information, but don't go too far. Before too long, they'll want a chance to pipe up and add their point of view.

"You talk"

Now, give them the opportunity to have a chat to the person next to them. Many *good* speakers fail to be *great*, because they don't give the audience this opportunity. When done well, lots of little discussions break out around the room as people discuss the points that have been delivered so far. Do they understand them? Do they agree? Do they want to extend the ideas further? Each discussion will have its own flavour and direction, and the people in them will be the ones guiding that process. After a while, it will be time to bring the room together and focus the discussion in the direction you want to head.

"We talk"

Now you take three comments from the floor from people who want to share something about what they've just discussed. It might be in support of one of your points, or seeking some clarification about the topic. It gives the audience a chance to contribute to the discussion, and it gives you the chance to tune into the frequency of your audience. The responses you get from people in the audience will give you a great indication of what's landing in the room.

THREE LEVELS OF INTERACTION

Working the room is designed to involve your audience in your presentation. It can range from them laughing and relating to what you say by internally interacting with your message, right through to joining you on stage and physically engaging in the presentation.

Interactive pieces can occur in three ways: in the minds of the audience—"imagine yourself..."; individually—"grab a pen and write down..."; or in groups—"turn to the person next to you and...". You can also have low energy exercises—"write down three things..." and high energy exercises—"thank you sir, come and join me on stage...". Plot those against each other and you are left with a six-place model. It looks like this:

	IN THEIR MINDS	BY THEMSELVES	WITH OTHERS
HIGH ENERGY	2	4	6
LOW ENERGY	1	3	5

There are six places on the model—six types of interaction you can plan into your presentation. You're not limited to six interactions overall, of course, you can have multiple interactive 'bits' that fit each type. You might have ten or fifteen low-risk, internal interactions you use at various stages in the presentation for example (these are type 1 interactions).

Here are some examples of interactive exercises you could use in a presentation, and where they fit into the model:

Type	Exercise
1	Ask an open ended rhetorical question.
1	Say "Remember a time when you felt like everything was 'in flow'".
2	Lead the audience through a guided visualisation.
2	Say "Remember a time when you were scared or felt a sense of failure".
3	Ask them to write down their expectations for the session.
3	Ask them to mentally rehearse what they might say at the next staff meeting.
4	Invite an audience member on stage.
4	Put two seats on stage and 'hot seat' an audience member's learnings.
5	Invite the audience to say hello to people around them and swap cards
5	Have the audience participate in a roundtable problem-solving session
6	Have groups present findings of discussions to the whole room
6	Get the entire room singing and dancing

Great audience interaction is about respecting the audience and doing things with a purpose. Well-designed interactive pieces are often the most powerful part of a great presentation, but they always fall flat if they don't have a purpose for the audience. The audience will do nearly anything you ask them, so long as you earn their trust. Some presenters use interaction for its own sake, and this is a short-lived strategy. Audience members giving them the benefit of the doubt may participate early and energetically, but they soon get wise to the fact that there is no point to the interaction and they resent being duped.

Only slightly better than interaction without purpose is interaction with a naff purpose, like the 'stand up and massage the shoulders of the person next to you' activity. Nobody enjoys being forced beyond their personal boundaries because a presenter told them to, and they'll be loath to participate again when further interactive activities are introduced. Interactive activities need to be linked to a learning outcome for the audience to appreciate them. They don't work as an 'ice breaker', that's what humour is for.

RAMP THE ROOM

Interaction needs to be progressive. The audience will give you a little trust to begin with. They'll offer you a limited amount of trust, which you can use to ask them to do something low risk. If the exercise is useful and has a purpose, their trust will grow and you can start to increase the amount of interaction.

Think of it like dating: You don't start a first date with, "Hey, let's get married, have three kids, and buy a house". You work up to that point, usually over a number of years. Instead you start with, "Would you like to share a coffee?" a much lower risk activity which your potential mate is much more likely to agree to.

Start with interaction that is comfortable, wait for the audience to accept and appreciate it, and as their trust in you grows, you can start to 'ramp the room' up to more energetic and higher risk activities. It's like riding a wave. As you surf the interaction in a room, you need to make minor adjustments along the way to keep things gliding along. Sometimes you have to wind things back a bit and slow down the pre-planned interactions to wait for the audience to catch up. Sometimes you can drop an activity altogether if you know it's going to flop; at other times, you should skip some of your low risk progressions if the room is in the palm of your hand and ready to rock. To be able to do this effectively, you need to have a clear awareness of the methods of interaction available to you as a presenter, and whether they sit on a higher or lower energy curve.

ANY QUESTIONS?

How many times have you heard someone come abruptly to the end of their presentation, to say "So, any questions?" It's like punctuating the end of a sentence with a giant ink blot. Generally met with stony silence, a few swivelling heads, and finally a smattering of awkward applause.

A masterful presenter who leads a conversation with the tribe, will want to give the audience a chance to add their voice to that conversation. We're not rubbishing the idea of a Q&A session entirely. Here are some tools and techniques that can be used to better manage the Q&A segments of your presentations, and allow you to work the room, harnessing the expertise and energy of the audience.

Be careful what you ask for

Don't ask for questions unless you're okay with having people question what you say. Be prepared for detractors, challengers, and those who want to drill down to see what lies behind your claim to authority. Remember that speakership is the great certainty filter. Anything you're unsure about will be exposed and interrogated when you say it in public.

Don't ask for questions alone

Invite the audience to interact through a three-tiered approach. Ask if anyone:

1. has any questions, or additional ideas
   they would like to contribute;

2. would like any clarifications, or to discuss previous ideas, or;

3. would simply like to make a statement, share their
   expertise, or highlight what they've learned.

Inviting a variety of contributions gives the audience a chance to truly rise into conversation. Even the name 'question and answer' sounds a bit like 'us and them'. It's not particularly inclusive. Give the audience a chance to converse with you, in whatever manner they feel compelled, and they will be much more likely to want to get involved.

Don't cold call for questions

Give the audience a chance to discuss their questions with the person next to them before you invite them to ask it in front of the entire room. Consider the fact that you were nervous prior to speaking, and you had days or weeks to prepare! How must they be feeling? At least give them a chance to ask their question aloud to one other person, so they can feel comfortable and assured that it's a contribution worth adding to the discussion, before they commit to saying it to the whole room.

Don't wait till it's over

Set up a question-and-answer session about three-quarters of the way through your talk. It's hard to finish on a high when you have to answer questions. In a 60 minute speech, you might start questions at the 40 to 45 minute mark and plan to spend five minutes or so, before turning your focus back to the key points of your message and concluding in the fashion you want to.

Listen slow and answer fast

When someone is asking a question, turn down the pace a little. Whatever they say, you should restate it clearly for the benefit of the audience, so listen harder than you normally do. Often the peak adrenaline state while speaking can cause you to appear impatient. Remember, just because you're 'on' and in the zone mentally, the audience may not be. To you, it may seem like watching grass grow to have to wait for an audience member to get their question out, but it's essential to building effective Q&A, so adjust your pace.

Answer the better question

Audience members often ask convoluted and detail-specific questions which, whilst they might be entirely valid, don't really serve the room. Because you restate every question for the benefit of the audience, you have an opportunity to reframe the question to make it more beneficial for the room, and make the asker look good (and you should *always* make the asker look good!).

Your restatement of their question might begin something like "If I'm understanding you correctly, you're asking about how <big idea> affects <other big idea>, and how you might deal with that in your case? Okay great, so I think…". This is another example of why your work in pink sheets is so crucial. If you're always mired in detail, a single question from a crotchety audience member can derail your presentation and distract the focus of your audience. By working in contextual themes and overarching ideas, you can always pull an ill-directed discussion back on track by reframing the question to the advantage of yourself and the tribe.

TUNE INTO THE ROOM

The best way to elevate the energy and engagement in a room is to match their energy and slowly increase it to where you want it to be. A quiet, reserved audience will *not* react positively to a raging maniac taking the stage. Google any speech by Steve Ballmer, former CEO of Microsoft, for an eye-opening demonstration. Not recommended first thing in the morning! If you want to take the audience on a journey with you, you have to start at their level.

You need to get on the same frequency as your audience.

This is particularly true for leaders who are called upon to address challenging situations in your organisations. Perhaps you're delivering what might be perceived as 'bad news', maybe you're addressing difficult issues. We're all familiar with the idea of trying to get on the same wavelength as another person. If a room is exhibiting a predominant mood—say of anger—any attempt to alter this mood would be best started by meeting the anger yourself, joining the audience on that level, and *then* lift the tone by one, to turn the frequency up a notch. If the room is already hyped and humming then your energy needs to match that. Don Beck introduced this idea of meeting and matching people as a key to managing major cultural change projects. You can read more on this by searching for work on memes and memetic evolution.

ALTER THE ATMOSPHERE

There are a few different ways to meet and alter the mood of the room, and it's a good idea to practice these strategies so you'll have them available to you when you find yourself in a 'hostile environment'—it *will* happen, one day, and it *doesn't* need to end in disaster!

1. The first strategy is to come right out and name the prevailing mood. Using the feel/felt/found approach is a good way to approach this. "I understand how you may be feeling (name it) I have felt the same (recall time) but I have found that (insert reframe or preferred state or outcome)". People appreciate honesty. Having the chutzpah to stand at the front of the room and accept the existing mood is something the audience will generally respect and respond to.

2. You can tell a story with the existing mood woven into the opening scene, which concludes several levels above where you started. It allows the use of both humour and drama to slowly lift the energy in the room and bring it to a higher place.

3. Ask courageous questions. Challenge the room. Display courage, and invite them to reflect that courage back to you. Naming the elephant in the room and challenging your audience to own what's happened and have courageous conversations works.

Working the room is like dancing with the audience. You, as the presenter, have got to be into it as much as they are. You need to lead, and step confidently into the interaction as though you are certain it's going to work; no half-measures, no room for doubt. Benjamin Zander, an inspiring example of speakership in action, says it is the role of the leader to have absolutely no doubt that the audience will do exactly what is asked of them. Together you are co-creating an experience that is entertaining and educational. By involving the audience in your presentation you increase the likelihood they'll remember your message and share it with the wider tribe.

PRINCIPLE 7

Choose your state

One of the great challenges of public speaking is bringing an engaging and energetic version of yourself to the stage in a way that feels genuinely authentic. As intangible as it is, who you're *being* while you speak matters as much—or more—than what you're saying. We've touched on a number of tools and techniques you can use to help amplify yourself. As the person up the front, you're responsible for setting the energy of the room. What this boils down to is state management.

State management is about controlling what's going on inside you. It's about choosing composure when accepting chaos would be easier. When you speak you are often highly charged, it's difficult not to be with so much adrenalin running through your system. The key is to be able to respond rather than react. To choose who and how you will *be*.

You have the ability to influence the mood of the room and sometimes you'll see your internal state reflected back to you in the response of the audience. There are no bad audiences, just bad experiences. A presenter who feels that the audience was boring was probably bored themselves. A presenter who finds the audience angry or hostile was probably stirred up or frustrated. If you're able to come in clean then you're better able to assess where the audience is at, independent from anything you're projecting onto them.

That's not to say that you won't have bad days. Of course you will; we all do. The difference is, if your work that day is to present to a room full of people, you are required to get over it and get on with the presentation. Public speaking creates a mirror in which you see in the audience an amplified version of what is going on inside of you. Masterful presentation means being able to choose your state.

At the very beginning of this book we talked about the path to mastery of speakership being the ultimate personal development vehicle, and this ability to manage state might be the most challenging—and most rewarding—stage in that journey.

Consider for a moment whether you at this moment have total control of your state. Can you simply choose to be relaxed, confident, and ready to perform? What happens if you're suffering from a flu? Or if someone makes a negative comment just before you begin? Or if your slideshow file is corrupted? Or the conference organiser tells you they're running overtime and you only have a 15 minute slot? Or the CEO mentions right before you present your pitch that the budgets have been slashed?

If you're to become a world class presenter, if you're to truly master speakership, you need to be able to take all kinds of distractions and setbacks in your stride, your internal state unaffected by the things around you that are outside of your control. You can't allow circumstance to have power over you. Speakership is the ultimate personal development vehicle, and the confidence and focus that comes from being the master of your internal state is possibly its greatest reward.

So, what can you do? As much as we'd like to, very few people are able to just 'choose' their state. Most people live in a state of reaction, unable to choose their response in a given set of circumstances. Personal development guru Dr Steven Covey was asked which of his 7 Habits of Highly Effective People was the most important. He chose *Habit 1 - Be Proactive*. He says it is "undoubtedly the foundation for leadership... because it begins with the mindset 'I am responsible for me, and I can choose'. The key to being proactive is remembering that between stimulus and response there is a space. The space represents our choice—how we will choose to respond to any given situation, person, thought or event."

Mastery of state means having the ability to make good choices, no matter what. It means to be in control of what's happening within you, so you can impact what's happening around you. The foundation of mastering this principle is a firm decision on your part. You must *decide* that you will become the master of your own state and accept total responsibility for your internal dialogue.

With that decision made, here are three steps for managing your state effectively.

1. Prepare your mind

2. Prepare your body

3. Control your inputs

1. PREPARE YOUR MIND

Be mindful

The body of evidence detailing the benefits of mindful meditation is large and growing. Neuroscientific studies show that mindful meditation increases focus and self-control while reducing stress and anxiety. A regular mindfulness practice alters the physical and chemical composition of the brain and equips it to maintain greater control of state.

Mindfulness is the ability to live in the moment. It gives you the ability to avoid agonising about the mistakes of the past, and the anxiety of anticipating possible mistakes in the future. It gives you the ability to focus on the situation at hand and bring all of yourself to bear. It's a shortcut to mastering this principle and mastering speakership.

Formerly the domain of religious monks and yogis, mindfulness has definitely made its way into the mainstream. While enthusiastic proponents spend weeks or months at meditation retreats and hours a day meditating, even a small commitment to mindfulness training can have a positive impact on your ability to choose your state. Being mindful on stage means you can move on quickly from anything that might go wrong. If technology fails, or your jokes don't land you are able to release the negative thoughts about this that might affect the next few minutes of your presentation. Mindfulness allows you to stay in the present and focus only on the point you are making in the present moment.

There are a number of guided meditation companions available for download. This is a quick and easy way to introduce mindfulness training into your life with a time commitment as little as ten minutes a day. The Smiling Mind app (smilingmind.com.au) is one great example.

Focus on the game plan

Leading sports psychologist Sean Richardson says high performers focus on actions, *not* results. There's no value in letting yourself imagine how the presentation might go. There's no benefit to be found in thinking about whether the audience will enjoy it or not. Richardson says that champion footballers focus on things like following the team plan, fulfilling their responsibility in defence, working hard on offence, and making space for their teammates. They don't focus on how many goals they will (or won't) kick.

As a speaker getting ready to perform, you too need to focus on actions, not results. Prepare your mind for the mechanics of what you are about to do, rather than any potential outcome. You need to know that you've done the work and have your game plan (be it a speech on an envelope, or a well prepared slide deck) formulated in advance and ready to go. You can visualise the delivery of your opening remarks, or silently step through the gestures that accompany each of your key messages.

By focusing on your actions you ensure that you are detached from the result. If you've done the preparation and you know you're ready, you can step onto the stage comfortable that you've done everything you can, and that whatever happens, happens.

Establish an anchor

Athletes, actors, surgeons, pilots, TV presenters have been known to use the technique of anchoring to get themselves into a performance state. As a leader it's worthwhile developing an anchored gesture you can use before and during your presentation to bring yourself back to a state that works for you, not against you.

Advocates of neurolinguistic programming posit that we can access high performance states by setting up an anchor.

To create an anchor, think back to a time where you were in flow, truly happy, at the top of your game. You might have achieved something tremendous, been completely at peace or have been 'in the zone'. As you reflect, remember in vivid detail how you felt, how your body felt—your stance, your face, your fingers. Think about the sounds, the smells, the sights that were around you. You can 'anchor' that feeling by compressing everything you felt at the time into a tiny gesture like the squeezing of your thumb against your forefinger or the clicking of your fingers.

Whenever you want to summons that feeling again, to rapidly place yourself in that state of high performance you simply perform the anchoring gesture and allow the supercomputer that is your brain to recreate the circuits and chemistry of that state.

On stage whenever you feel yourself starting to falter, or your energy and enthusiasm levels dropping you can very subtly perform your gesture without your audience even knowing, and in doing so reset your state.

2. PREPARE YOUR BODY

Our bodies are finely tuned machines, and like high performance racing cars they benefit enormously from good quality fuel. There are simple, yet crucially important things you can do to ensure that you are in the best physical condition for every presentation you give.

Eat right

Protein, not carbohydrates, will help you remain mentally alert. Watch your caffeine intake. It's a diuretic and makes you need to go to the toilet and increases your chances of a dry mouth. Plan your day, and force food down if you are nervous. When you are on adrenaline, your body shuts down the hunger response and the last thing you want to do is eat. Do it, or you will end up with a sugar crash and lose the mental energy required to stay in state.

Exercise on the day

Excess nerves and mental over-stimulation compounds the amount of cortisol in your body. Cortisol is like the back-up fuel of the adrenal system, and too much cortisol can make you angry, sad, afraid or guilty. These four emotions are state-killers for a speaker. Some vigorous exercise on the day of the speech can help take the excess stress hormones out of your system.

Breathe deeply

As you prepare for a presentation you'll want to be in an optimal state. Controlling your biochemistry is challenging. Adrenalin rushes can be brutal so in addition to exercise it's a good idea to breathe consciously in preparation for your speech. Every 15 minutes or so take a moment to draw a few deep breaths. This helps keep you calm and enables a recalibration of your system.

If ever you feel yourself getting wound up on stage, the simple act of breathing deeply, through your diaphragm can help you choose your state. You can give the audience a long look, a lengthened smile, a dramatic pause and as you do so, be very conscious of filling your diaphragm with air and slowly releasing it. The extra oxygen into your blood and brain works to calm you and you both figuratively and literally lengthen the gap between stimulus (what you are feeling, experiencing, what has just happened) and response (getting back into a state that serves the room).

Move to improve

Tony Robbins coined the phrase 'your motion creates emotion' and his workshops are full of exercises that explore this idea. If you find yourself in an unhelpful state, get moving. Run on the spot, stretch, take long strides as you walk, stand up super straight and tall. All these physical actions send a message to the brain about how you should be feeling. If you're on stage, get moving. Take a walk to the other side of the stage. Make an expansive gesture with your arms so that you are literally open to the room. You get to choose how you move, and correspondingly, how you feel.

3. CONTROL YOUR INPUTS

On the day of your presentation you'll have a bunch of competing interests. Your children might still need to be taken to school, emails will still come flooding into your inbox, your phone will still ring.

Taking charge of your inputs is about creating space before you speak so that the inputs you receive are those that will serve you, inputs that help you choose your state.

Take care of yourself

You could choose music that you think would suit your audience, or get them pumped up ready for your presentation. Or, you could remember that their energy will simply be a reflection of the energy that you bring to stage, so instead you should choose music that suits you, and gets you in the right state ready for your presentation. Have the MC read an introduction about you that gets you pumped up and excited to present. Do whatever you must to get yourself in the zone.

The key thing to remember about managing your state is to remember that it's actually not about you. You're choosing an internal state because it serves the room to do so. Don't let people disrupt your state management routine because you don't want to seem rude or selfish by sending them away. As a presenter in service of the tribe, it would be selfish and rude to step on stage in a poor mental state. In looking after yourself you are looking after the room. You should prioritise it very, very highly.

You're on before you're on

It's important to realise that your performance starts long before you step on stage. Just as a sportsperson has a warm-up routine to ensure they're ready to perform when the siren sounds, you need to have a block of time carved out before your performance to give yourself the opportunity to ensure you're mentally ready.

It's equally important—perhaps more so—to ensure the people around you understand that you're not to be interrupted or disturbed once your mental preparation is underway. Get all the administrative and technical details sorted out long before you begin, so that you're free to spend the final ten or fifteen minutes reviewing your 'speech on an envelope', rehearsing sections of your presentation in your head, and mentally preparing yourself to give a great performance.

Until you develop the ability to choose your state no matter the situation, pre-speech rituals can help you engineer the right state. Some people clean their teeth before they speak no matter where or when they are presenting. You might like to have a shower, or listen to a particular song on your iPod.

Michael Jordan wore his North Carolina shorts under his Chicago Bulls uniform every time he played. Your rituals might take a while to develop, and really all you're trying to do is identify and replicate the process that helps you get into the right mental state. There's no right or wrong way to do it, so make your rituals meaningful for you.

Be your own barometer

Before you speak you may have been given a heads up about the audience and what they're like. Be careful. Whoever is giving you that heads up will have their own interpretation of what's going on. Like all masterful presenters, you will always endeavour to read your room and adjust your presentation accordingly. The problem is, it's possible to misread situations and believe things are going better (or worse) than they are. Don't assume you know too much about an audience. Stay a little detached and self-referring with your state. Remember, if you feel good, chances are they will too.

See the lighter side

In any challenging situation, if you can see the funny side, you can almost immediately get out of a funk or an unproductive emotional state and choose a better one. The fact is that every situation can be interpreted negatively or positively. The cliché "What doesn't kill you makes you stronger" does a poor job of capturing what is actually a very important idea.

Every situation provides an opportunity for growth. Every situation can be interpreted as a positive experience if you choose it to be. Controlling your inputs mean you don't need to be a victim of your circumstances, and you don't need to give your power over to other people.

Choosing to interpret all of life's challenges as positive experiences can have enormous flow-on benefits for you and the people around you. People that shy away from difficult situations often miss out on learning the most important lessons that come from such moments, and therefore don't gain the toughness and experience that lends itself to great leadership.

If your speakership journey is driven by a desire to lead then your ability to feel genuinely positive in difficult situations, and to project that positivity outwardly, will contribute enormously to your ability to gain the trust of your tribe.

PRINCIPLE 8

Expand your awareness

Expanding your awareness is key to mastering speakership and is divided into two distinct parts: awareness in observation, and awareness in action.

AWARENESS IN OBSERVATION

We talked in the introduction about the idea of 'seeing behind the curtain' at the magic show. Awareness in observation is the act of watching every speech and presentation with a discerning and critical eye. The fact is that simply expanding your knowledge of what is possible expands your capabilities.

Some say that "What you don't know can't hurt you", but where personal growth is concerned "What you don't know you can't access" would be a statement closer to the truth. Expanding the horizons of your understanding immediately and irrevocably expands the horizons of your performance.

Each time you observe a new technique used in a presentation, that technique becomes available to you. Sure, you may not execute it perfectly on your first attempt, but simply being aware of its existence is the majority of the battle won. From there it's just a case of practice.

When the opportunity to watch a presenter in action arises, your ability to observe what's really going on is key to expanding your potential. Look for the contextual themes of the presentation, the focus of the presenter, the energy in the room and the presenter's ability to dance with the audience. Some of your most profound leaps forward will happen not while you're presenting yourself, but when you're sitting anonymously in the crowd, observing a presentation that introduces a new level of clarity to your own definition of speakership mastery.

Wear perspecticles

As your awareness expands you'll be able to filter many different situations through the lens of speakership. It's as though you start to see the world through spectacles that give you a whole new perspective. Here are five ways to take advantage of your increasing awareness:

1. Read more. Seek out case studies, stories, and examples that you can use when you speak. Notice the way the stories are constructed and study the use of language.

2. Go to live comedy shows. Sit in the audience and notice how the comedians work the crowd, use gestures, control their voices and share anecdotes.

3. Attend live theatre. Even one or two live dramatic shows will switch you on to the subtleties of body movement and the nuance of gesture to convey meaning.

4. Follow the gurus. Whenever you get the chance to be in the audience of a speakership expert, take it. The 'topic' may be of no interest, their audience not your tribe. Turn up and watch everything the gurus do to serve their audiences. Observe their state management, their animation, and interaction.

5. Interrogate your impact. If you're in conversation with friends and they laugh at a story you're telling,

run an internal interrogation. Ask yourself what you did that made them laugh? A witty anecdote? A wry observation well delivered? An over the top caper complete with action replays and siren sound effects? Notice the impact you have on those around you. Your impact provides clues as to how you can bring authentic humour and entertainment to the stage.

Expanding your awareness in observation unlocks a path to rapid and exponential personal growth.

AWARENESS IN ACTION

Awareness in action—the 'third eye' that characterises masterful presenting—is the ability to speak with confidence whilst undergoing an almost out-of-body experience. You're able to observe the speech, the audience, and the energy in the room as though you're not the speaker but an impartial observer. Cynthia Montgomery, Harvard professor and author of *The Strategist*, describes it like a dancer, "Being able to watch from the balcony, and see the dance".

This ability is like an extension of your empathy. Humans in a shared experience generate a kind of collective energy among the group. We have an incredible ability to sense how everyone else in the room is feeling and tune ourselves into that energy level. Whatever is happening around us can bring that shared energy up, and bring it back down again.

The time when this is most obvious is at concerts and festivals. The energy in the crowd ebbs and flows with the energy coming from the stage. A masterful artist can bring the crowd to a frenzy, or ease them back down again to rest and get ready to go again, conducting the energy of the experience like the maestro commands an orchestra.

The ability to monitor the energy of the crowd and simultaneously manage it and shape it while presenting from the stage is mastery. When you fully engage awareness in action you become the maestro at the front of the room. Your words and actions are chosen as carefully as the conductor would choose the flourish to the horn section to bring them to life.

You'll be able to sense when the audience is turned on by your inspirational introduction and ready to be shown the map your strategy lays out. You'll know when their energy is down and they want some simple, low-risk mental exercises to build their engagement; and when their energy is up and they're really ready to rock and roll with you.

More importantly, you'll know how to move them from one energy level to another. If the audience feels particularly flat, you'll use humour and drama to build the energy in the room. Conversely, if the energy reaches fever-pitch and you know they'll need a break in order to make it to the end, you'll introduce a pause in proceedings that gives them time to catch their breath.

Awareness in action requires you to get so comfortable with your material and so practiced in your presentation skills that you can perform them while barely thinking about it. Once you get to the point where you're so practiced, so polished that the presenting almost takes care of itself, then you can leave your body behind, and take your consciousness up to the balcony to observe the dance.

This is not some pseudo-scientific hokum, by the way. We're not suggesting you'll have a literal out-of-body experience. This awareness is a skill, and one that can be developed. Let's describe the science behind this 'third eye awareness', both what it is and how you can acquire it, so you can fast-track your rise to mastery.

Of all the organs in the human body, by far the least understood is the brain. In his bestselling book *Thinking, Fast and Slow*, Nobel prize winning psychologist Daniel Kahneman details our current best understanding of the process by which the human mind works. It's an absolutely fascinating read and certainly provides food for thought.

The complete process of what is physically (electrically and chemically) happening in the brain is far from understood, but from a functional perspective, it's as though we are guided by two completely different thinking systems. Two separate 'agents' in our minds, which are connected and related, and yet very distinct from each other. As you might guess from the title of Kahneman's book, one system thinks quickly (he calls it System 1), and one thinks comparatively slowly (System 2).

System 1 thinking happens without your effort, or your control. It provides data to your consciousness with incredible speed. It's the system that monitors the sounds in a crowded room and alerts you when you hear your name. It's the system which controls your breathing and blinking. It's the system that lets you coordinate the accelerator, clutch and gear-stick when driving, and more importantly, that rapidly sends your foot to the brakes in an emergency. Importantly for those interested in the art of oration, it's the system which collects the words you need to articulate your thoughts, and also controls your diaphragm, throat, vocal chords and mouth as you speak.

System 2 thinking happens with your effort, and under your control. It performs higher-order computation, and processes complicated concepts. It's the system that learns new skills. It's the system that writes emails, essays and books (but doesn't control the fingers as you touch type, which is System 1's domain). It's the system that considers political policies. It's the system we use to make considered, conscientious decisions. System 2 can deliberately wrest control of many tasks usually the domain of System 1. You can breathe or blink on command, for instance.

Unfortunately, nervous tension has the ability to cause a degree of havoc. It can interrupt the normal flow of information in the brain and cause System 2 to start second-guessing things. You've probably seen a professional tennis player reach match point and serve a double-fault. They've served literally thousands upon thousands of bullet-like serves perfectly in training—and even in the very match they're playing—and yet the nervous tension created by the pressure of the final point causes a glitch. Why does it happen?

A tennis serve, once practiced, is a task performed by System 1. But now, under the pressure of match point, System 2 gets nervous, and tries to wrest back control. Unfortunately, System 2 hasn't done thousands of hours of practice like System 1 has, so it's nowhere near as good at controlling the serve. The result is a double fault.

Insofar as Systems 1 and 2 are concerned, speaking is analogous to a tennis serve. System 2 makes decisions about what to say based on higher-order thinking (like the context of the discussion, other points that have already been made, etc.), then System 1 performs the task of collecting all the necessary words in order and saying them out loud. In low pressure situations it happens flawlessly, almost all of the time. When chatting with your family at the dinner table, you don't regularly stumble over your words, or lose your train of thought.

State management, then, is largely about controlling your System 2 thinking. It can be used to your advantage, observing the room; or to your detriment, interrupting the natural flow of your speech.

On that basis, awareness in action is really just the ability to control your state. To ensure that System 1 does what it is supposed to (control your actual speaking) while System 2 concentrates on what it should—consider the next major point you wish to make, monitor the energy in the room, watch yourself from out the front so you can adjust your body language etc.

Trust yourself. Trust that your knowledge, your research and your preparation has given your System 1 brain the tools it needs to speak confidently on your topic. Doing so gives System 2, your analytical self, the ability to observe your dance with the audience "from the balcony".

Awareness in action is the tool by which your engagement and interaction with the audience is leveraged. Once you learn to choose and control your own state, your ability to focus your System 2 thinking on the state of the room will grow rapidly.

The idea of awareness in action can seem a little esoteric, and yet there are also very practical considerations that masterful speakers take care of seamlessly and without fuss. These include:

- Monitoring the temperature of the room and how comfortable the audience is

- Instinctively knowing that the audience is done with sitting down and need an activity that involves getting up and moving around

- Ensuring that the microphone volume and playback volume for video clips are set at appropriate levels and making adjustments throughout the presentation if need be

- Monitoring the lighting so that any slides are easily seen, and the audience can take notes if they wish

Expanded awareness leads to speakership mastery, where you can expertly redesign your presentations on the fly to suit the energy of the room and the disposition of the audience. You'll become more than a presenter. You'll become a maestro, with the audience as your orchestra, each of them responding to your every word and gesture. Your energy will guide their experience and the memory of how you made them feel will last with them for a long time. Mastering the expansion of your awareness is a leadership essential.

PRINCIPLE 9

Get out of the way

There are moments of perfection. Moments of pure joy where every tiny comment you make to a crowd has them laughing, where a poignant story silences the room and all anyone can hear is the sound of their own heart beating. Moments where you land a key point and it's as though light bulbs literally turn on in the eyes of your audience. There's a collective 'Wow', a shared understanding and a renewed sense of community within a room of people.

These are the moments a leader who speaks lives for. Professional speakers know the feeling and, like a surfer finally catching a wave after hours of nothing, that one moment is enough to keep you going, week after week, audience to audience.

In these moments there is no ego, no self-doubt, no compensatory over confidence. There's just a shared experience that is much greater than the sum of its parts.

How can we master this? How can we increase the chances that our presentations will contain moments like this?

We have to get out of the way. We have to get out of our own way. When you stand and speak in service of the tribe it's no longer about you. You're essentially a vessel for the messages that matter. You can only be truly free to deliver those when you detach from all the thoughts that fill your head about yourself. It's the destination in the journey of focus from I to You to We.

When you get out of the way, you create space to just be with the audience in an authentic, fully present dance. It's hard to do, because our natural instincts are so focused on caring about what others think of us. The irony is of course that the less we care what others think of us, the more likely that they do.

DEALING WITH CRITICS

As part of your journey towards speakership mastery, you will have to decide how to deal with the naysayers, snipers, and abuse 'from the cheap seats'. If you are willing to stand up in front of a crowd and 'throw rocks' at something (or someone), then you must also be willing to withstand the criticism that comes your way as a result.

Of course, most leaders are willing to have their ideas held to scrutiny—and we would hope that you fit that category—but there are two kinds of criticism that get levelled at even the best speakers and leaders, and you should deal with them in very different ways.

The first kind of criticism is valid, considered, and constructive, and you should actively seek out this kind of feedback. If you hope to change the world then your message will need to be powerful, compelling, and *true*. If you're advocating to solve a problem with a solution that simply won't work in practice, what's the point in assembling a tribe behind you to put it into action? What good will come of convincing a whole bunch of people to come with you on a journey to failure?

For this reason alone, constructive criticism should be treated like gold. It is through the rigour of defending your ideas against constructive criticism that you can tweak and improve your message until it becomes the clear choice for anyone faced with the problems you know how to solve. If you never have to justify your opinion through some healthy scepticism, you can never be sure your ideas truly have merit. So the first kind of criticism—valid, considered, and constructive—is a welcome and positive influence on the development of your message, and your development as a leader. Hillary Rodham Clinton says she tries to take criticism seriously, not personally.

The second kind of criticism is not, unfortunately, a welcome or positive influence. Being brave enough to stand at the front of a room and share your message with the world imparts you with a little bit of celebrity. Celebrity can be a good thing, in many ways, but it can also be a very bad thing. It's important for a prospective leader to learn to discern real, constructive criticism from the negative and useless attacks that may come your way thanks to even a small amount of celebrity energy. As modern-day philosopher Taylor Swift said—haters gonna hate.

A percentage of small-minded people will always begrudge those who have distinguished themselves from their peers, no matter how meritorious the elevation. Australians call it Tall Poppy Syndrome, and it's thought to be derived from their convict heritage generating a suspicion of authority. The Irish too consider it a peculiarly Irish character flaw.

Unfortunately, celebrities—along with people of status or authority—are treated with a degree of undeserved disdain from a minority of the population no matter where in the world they are. Bottom line, to a small subset of the population the very fact that you are willing to stand up and speak out makes you a target for unfair critique.

As a speaker and a leader, you will almost certainly weather some unfounded and unfair criticism and personal attacks at some point in your career. You need to be bulletproof because some negative people in the audience will treat you just as they would a celebrity on the cover of a trashy magazine—'fair game' for spiteful, non-constructive criticism. You have to accept this and accept that ignoring it is all you can do to deal with it.

When exhibited on the internet, we describe this behaviour as 'trolling'—generally described as a deliberate attempt to get an emotional response from someone. On the internet, the best advice to remedy the situation is simply "Don't feed the troll". That is—don't engage with them, don't even honour their comment with the respect of the time it takes to reply, because it simply doesn't deserve it.

In life, as in the internet, this holds true. If you know a criticism levelled at you or your message is deliberately inflammatory, designed to hurt you personally or elicit an emotional reaction from you, the best course of action is simply to ignore it. Don't offer it the dignity of a response, nor give the person in question the satisfaction of throwing you off your course. Simply ignore it, forget it, and move on.

CONTROLLING YOUR FOLDBACK MIX

If you've ever seen a band sound check before a gig you'll hear the lead singer asking for a particular mix of foldback. The foldback is the music that the musicians hear through their earpieces and is often quite different to the mix the audience will hear. "Johnny, I've got too much guitar, I need more piano". Getting the mix right for each band member is an important part of the set up. In order to perform at their best, different members of the band need a personalised mix of foldback.

As you step into speakership you can also afford to be selective about where you take feedback from, and *no-one* should take feedback from *everyone*. It's not that you want to surround yourself with people who only say nice things and tell you what they think you want to hear. The idea is to seek feedback that accelerates your growth while maintaining your sense of self-worth and passion for what you're doing so surround yourself with people who can provide this.

The flipside is, of course, that *no-one* can be the leader for *everyone*. No matter how great your message, no matter how committed to service you are, no matter how humbly you accept responsibility, your message won't be for everyone. If what you have is not what they need right now, it doesn't mean you should stop, or give too much attention to their feedback. It most likely means they need to find another leader, or a different tribe.

YOU DON'T MATTER, THEY DON'T CARE, AND THEY'RE NOT LISTENING

The truth is, committing to the speakership journey is not for everyone. It takes courage and conviction to succeed in the spotlight. It takes a degree of self-belief and self-confidence that isn't found in all people. In seeking out this challenge and committing to pursuing mastery, the likelihood is that you possess a gift that makes you unique in some way or another.

You might be uncommonly insightful, intelligent, creative or perceptive. You might have an idea you think could change a community or an industry (or the whole world). You've got something that sets you apart from the crowd, and now you need to be heard.

At which point the hard truth sets in. Some people are going to love you and your message. Some people aren't. And that's okay.

You may indeed be possessed of a unique intelligence or a world-changing idea, but be warned that a healthy dose of humility never goes astray. The greatest sin a speaker can commit is to overestimate your own importance, and the audience can be lightning-quick to judge.

One of the biggest mistakes we can make as leaders is to assume that we are interesting, or that our position entitles us to respect. Speaking in public is a constant process of working for the attention of your audience, trying with all your faculties to compete for a share of mind. The human mind thinks far faster than you can ever speak, so any given member of the audience can mentally wander off into their own thoughts during your presentation. You have to treat their attention as the most valuable thing in the world. When it comes to spreading messages that matter—it is.

So a useful mantra when shooting for mastery is: *You don't matter, they don't care, and they're not listening.* Of course, this statement isn't literally true:

- It's not that you actually don't matter, it's that you don't matter *first*.

- It's not that they actually don't care, it's that you haven't yet given them a *reason* to.

- It's not that they're actually not listening, but you have to ensure you're speaking *their* language.

Effective leadership is mobilising people to act. If you accept this to be true then the logical extension is that effective leadership is not about you, it's about the tribe. Any time you get self-centred or self-absorbed, you've strayed from the path of effective leadership.

In his book *Leaders Eat Last*, Simon Sinek explains that in most cultures the leader gets all kinds of privileges; the best tent, the nicest horse and the strongest husband. But all of this comes with an emotional contract that you, as the leader, won't be self-centred, that you won't take from the tribe.

The metaphor of eating last is symbolic of your delayed gratification in an act of service. Speaking is the live test of leadership orientation. If you are full of *you* when you speak, you have failed to honour this ancient contract.

It probably feels confronting to think that you would put all this effort into your presentation—weeks of preparation preceded by years of research and practice—only to be told of the audience that you don't matter, they don't care, and they're not listening. It is confronting! You're not just putting yourself out there, you're bringing an *amplified* version of yourself to stage, exposing your true essence for all to see, and yet... they don't care?

How can this be? Is it right? Is it fair? Possibly not, but that doesn't matter. No-one changes the world without taking a risk. Your willingness to put your ideas in the spotlight under the scrutiny of public opinion is admirable, but it doesn't give you the *right* to the attention or respect of the audience. Every time you speak you are *auditioning* for a leadership position. When you speak, it is your job to exhort, convince, and persuade the tribe to make you their leader. Operating from the assumption that they already follow you is a terrible mistake, no matter what your job title is.

You don't matter, they don't care, and they're not listening is a mantra to remind yourself that every moment you spend on stage is a moment you need to spend serving the tribe. You must operate from the assumption that the statement is true because to do otherwise is to set a course for failure.

Every individual life is complex and full, and if you're going to ask another person to give you their full attention, you have to give them a reason to care. If you speak to a person in their language, and give them a compelling reason that matters to them to care about what you're saying, *then* you may find that they believe you matter. Truly great leaders who devote their lives to service end up almost universally beloved, but they don't start from that assumption.

You don't matter, they don't care, and they're not listening is a mantra designed to remind you to get out of your own way. Using the spotlight to stroke your own ego or engage in therapy on stage is to flip the relationship of service between you and the audience. It is a great privilege to be given the opportunity to speak in public, and one that should be met with utmost humility.

To surrender yourself to speakership mastery is to set yourself free from the opinion of others. It means taking total responsibility for your ego and self-worth, for the good of the tribe. It means putting your very best work out into the world, and then detaching from the result. Sometimes the audience will adore you and be inspired to achieve amazing things. Inevitably, sometimes they won't. That's okay. Let it go.

Surrendering to your message, letting go of ego and stepping into service of the tribe is what enables you to lead from the front.

But first, begin

*'A book may give you excellent suggestions on how best to
conduct yourself in the water, but sooner or later you must
get wet, perhaps even struggle and be "half scared to death."
There are a great many "wetless" bathing suits worn at the
seashore, but no one ever learns to swim in them.
To plunge is the only way.'*

— Dale Carnegie

Sir Richard Branson, Warren Buffet, Sheryl Sandberg. Corporate leaders who have all talked openly about their journey to become better public speakers. Overcoming their fears, finding ways to deal with the unhelpful internal critical voice, and discovering how to make meaningful connections with their audiences, have been part of their personal stories

When you understand the nine practical principles, you're ready to walk the path to speakership mastery. Your very next presentation won't be perfect. In fact, you may never achieve perfection—but your awareness of yourself and the tension between what you're currently capable of and what you know is possible will create exponential improvement.

It's tempting to strive to be memorable. To be so unique and extraordinary that everyone in the audience is talking about you and your message.

The problem with striving to be unique is that your focus goes to the wrong place. A white belt in Taekwondo does not immediately try to perform a high spinning back kick, for that would almost certainly result in a clumsy fall, a total fail. A white belt practices simple, straight punches and low front kicks, until the fundamentals are bedded down and committed to muscle memory.

For leaders who speak, the price of entry to the game is relevance. If you do just one thing in your next speech, be relevant. In a world where all of human knowledge is a few clicks away, your audience is drowning in information. They need you to make sense of the madness, and curate the conversation so they know what matters most. Make sure the audience can answer these questions: why this topic, why this speaker, why now?

Once you've nailed relevance, you can take the time to be thorough. Research your topic deeply and agonise over what is important and what can be left out. Leave no stone unturned in seeking to educate your audience. Deliver every idea through rigorous full spectrum thinking. The audience will sense the depth of your expertise and appreciate your thorough approach.

Once you're thorough, you can take the time to be elegant. Elegance means delivering every point with pin-sharp precision. Each idea painstakingly crafted into memorable memes that can be easily understood and shared. Elegance means your contextual themes ring out through your presentation and affect the audience emotionally. They will find your presentation a profound and moving experience.

Finally, once you've provided relevant content, thoroughly researched and collated and elegantly delivered, you won't need to worry about being unique. You'll already be there. Standing on stage, bravely amplifying your imperfections in the service of the tribe, delivering messages that matter in ways that inspire people into action, you will be undeniably unique.

```
┌─────────────────────────────┐
│           Unique            │
└─────────────────────────────┘
              ▲
┌─────────────────────────────┐
│           Elegant           │
└─────────────────────────────┘
              ▲
┌─────────────────────────────┐
│          Thorough           │
└─────────────────────────────┘
              ▲
┌─────────────────────────────┐
│          Relevant           │
└─────────────────────────────┘
```

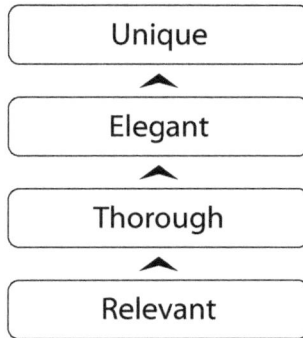

Start with relevance.

As we reach the conclusion, we think it's important to look to the future and the turning point reading this book could represent for you.

For some, it will be a curiosity; a book that made some interesting points which provoke some thoughts, and little more. If you belong to this group, we thank you for reading and hope you found it interesting and enjoyable. We'd love for you to keep this on your bookshelf to read again in five year's time. You can never be sure who you might be in future.

For some, it will be disruptor; a book which causes assumptions to be upset, raises some doubt, and starts a shift in mindset. If you belong to this group, we'd love you to let the content of this book sit in your consciousness for a while. Keep the book nearby, and read it again in a couple of months. We reckon the depth of content here is enough that the new insights you'll gain on the second pass through will be very beneficial and might unlock a new possible future for you.

For some, it will be like a starter's gun; a book which lays out the template for success that now appears within reach, and the only conceivable reaction is to leap out of the blocks and start running. If you belong to this group, well… get ready. Let's look to the future.

People	Business	Market
SIGNIFICANCE *Make a difference*	LEADERSHIP *Set the pace*	BRANDING *Be the market leader*
COMMUNICATION *Work with others*	PROMOTION *Educate others*	REPUTATION *Be well known*
CONFIDENCE *Take control*	IMPRESSION *Manage perceptions*	POSITIONING *Claim a space*

If you lay out the spectrum of influence you could create, from private to public, and then align that with the three layers of focus that have permeated this book—speaker, audience, tribe—you'll find yourself with this model.

PEOPLE

The most private group you can influence is the people around you. This includes your family, friends, colleagues, and extended networks. Let's unpack the benefits that flow from applying the 9 principles of speakership to yourself and the people around you.

The first benefit is confidence. Focus on yourself in the speakership framework and you will take control. You'll gain strength of conviction, clarity of purpose, and depth in your thinking.

Raising your focus brings an incredible increase in communication quality, and it's not just you sending messages outward. The change in mindset that comes with speakership creates a deep understanding of the way other people think and feel. You'll experience a profound shift in the way you work with others, a newfound ability to collaborate productively.

Finally, focus your speakership capabilities on serving the tribe around you and your will contribution will be significant. You *will* become a difference maker. People will live bigger, better lives just for the good fortune of having you in their network. You'll become a trusted mentor, with people assembling around you seeking help and guidance. When you seek to affect change, a whole tribe will be on your side to help.

BUSINESS

If you broaden the scope of influence out a rung, you turn your attention to a whole business. At the first layer, the narrow range of focus, this allows you to make an impression. A business implementing the speakership methodology has much greater control of perceptions surrounding the business. By controlling the language, both external perceptions and internal cultural memes are influenced and controlled by the leaders of the business.

Lifting focus to the audience enables the business to educate others. This manifests most heavily in promotion. An organisation with confident leaders sends messages out to the market that distinguish and elevate the business. They set the tone of the conversations being had in the business.

A business focused on the tribe becomes the leader of its class. A business operating in service of the tribe, lead out loud by masterful leaders, becomes the pacesetter of a whole industry. A yardstick by which all others are measured. A business so aligned with its customers that they are considered followers rather than consumers is more than an organisation, it's a cultural phenomenon.

MARKET

The most public end of the spectrum is the market, and the first consideration here is positioning. In controlling the words and language used to describe the business, you stake your claim to your space in the market. Positioning is a commercial essential and the fundamentals of speakership provide the platform for commanding and controlling market positioning.

Raising focus to the audience allows the business to build a solid reputation. Strong leadership develops relationships and understanding that cultivate a reputation that rings out through the market. Get known for what you do, and have the market tell your stories for you. Unlocking this capability makes your customers your own marketing department, spreading messages that matter through the market and building your reputation.

A business becomes a brand when it becomes a symbol of a particular culture. This transition happens when the leaders of the organisation connect to the tribe that follows them with a message that commands the context of their culture. For the people of the tribe, the brand becomes an important part of who they are, and they become not only evangelists but disciples for life.

It should seem clear at this point that the higher stages of the model translate directly into greater commercial success. An investment in accelerating the journey of yourself and your team towards speakership mastery is one that generates rapid returns.

If reading this book contributes to your future success, we are humbled by our contribution and grateful for the opportunity. If you would like our help to further accelerate your progress, we would be honoured to assist. We have committed our lives to the cause of changing the world by preaching and teaching speakership to speakers, small businesses, and large organisations the world over. We would be delighted to work with you, too.

Perhaps the most logical final question to ask is: What next?

Whether you're speaking to grow your leadership credentials, speaking to grow your business, or speaking *is* your business, the next step is to *take action*. Progress in the speaking world is rarely made academically. Don't sit there, say something!

speakership.com

NOTES

NOTES

www.ingramcontent.com/pod-product-compliance
Lightning Source LLC
Chambersburg PA
CBHW030509210326
41597CB00013B/841